GRAND CENTRAL
TERMINAL

GRAND CENTRAL TERMINAL

100 Years of a New York Landmark

By the New York Transit Museum and
Anthony W. Robins

Introduction by Tony Hiss

Stewart, Tabori & Chang, New York

Published in 2013 by Stewart, Tabori & Chang
An imprint of ABRAMS

Library of Congress Cataloging-in-Publication Data:

Robins, Anthony, author.
 Grand Central Terminal : 100 years of a New York
landmark / by the New
York Transit Museum and Anthony W. Robins ;
introduction by Tony Hiss.
    pages cm
  Includes bibliographical references and index.
 ISBN 978-1-58479-994-8 (hardback)
1. Grand Central Terminal (New York, N.Y.)—Pictorial
works. 2.
Railroad terminals—New York (State)—New York–
History. 3. Railroad
Terminals—Conservation and restoration—New York
(State)—New York. I. New York Transit Museum, author.
II. Title.
 NA6313.N4R63 2013
 725'.31097471—dc23
        2012020740

Editor: Jennifer Levesque
Designer: Topos Graphics
Production Manager: Kathy Lovisolo

The text of this book was composed in Grand Central,
and Sentinel.

Printed and bound in the United States
10 9 8 7 6 5 4 3

ABRAMS
THE ART OF BOOKS SINCE 1949

115 West 18th Street
New York, NY 10011
www.abramsbooks.com

Photograph by Frank English, 2009

Wayne Ehmann
1944-2010

This book is dedicated to our treasured
friend and colleague, who as design
manager and then chief architect at Metro-
North Railroad for twenty-five years, knew
and loved every inch of Grand Central

Dedication photograph by Frank English

Bottom photograph by Patrick Cashin

FOREWORD

I first started working at the Metropolitan Transportation Authority in January 1988, a month before Grand Central's 75th anniversary. The Terminal was a different place then, and the celebration walked a fine line between love and respect for a great building, and the unease our customers still felt in a borderline public space. At MTA Arts for Transit, we initiated some modest performing and visual arts programs in an effort to sway visitors' perceptions. And initial capital improvements uncovered the famous skylights and upgraded the roof. But it wasn't until major reconstruction of Grand Central was underway in the mid-1990s that New Yorkers began to sense a change. Scaffolding, brightly illustrated barricades, huge dramatic advertisements, and rerouted ramps filled the building with even more urgency than this center of the universe normally sustains. And when the newly restored, sparkling Grand Central was unveiled in 1998, it was a revelation. The building could be seen in a new light, through a new lens.

With this book, we hope to again show you Grand Central through a new lens. To dust off and relive its many uses over the decades; to marvel at the genius of inspiration and science that coincided to create it; to examine closeups of its many details; and to reveal its unseen infrastructure. Grand Central is a building full of secrets. In the following pages, we revisit what you may have forgotten or never knew about its past; the innovations that made it a modern marvel in its day and that give it a functional grace and simplicity that still presides. We bring you stories here about the many ways this great landmark has been used, and the history it has witnessed.

There have been many excellent books written on Grand Central. Our challenge was to show the Terminal from new angles without repeating what's been done so well by others. So we've omitted the story of the saving of Grand Central from the wrecker's ball. And we've omitted the long history of railroading in New York State, a complex industry that came, reached its heyday, and left us with at least one great rail station. What we do bring you is a collection of brilliant photos, most of which have not been published before, and the voices of journalists, writers and commentators who experienced Grand Central when it was truly a marvelous, new phenomenon.

Grand Central conjures meaning for those of us who've never stepped inside it, to those of us who pass through it or work in it every day. It is one of the city's great foundations, a monument that grounds New York and gives it permanence. We invite you to join us in celebrating the first hundred years of one of the world's great structures and saluting its advance into its next century.

Gabrielle Shubert
Director, New York Transit Museum

INTRODUCTION: GRAND CENTRAL'S GIFT TO NEW YORK

by Tony Hiss

There's a long history of things not lasting long in New York. On Grand Central Terminal's first day, February 2, 1913, the *New York Times* said that "people are asking, quite naturally, whether the great railroad station that is open today for the first time is the final, permanent structure, adequate to accommodate whatever future development may come." Quite naturally, because it was the third station on the same site in about forty years, and in New York, even things built to last are often not wanted for more than a little while. Case in point: the Hotel Belmont, seven years older than the current Grand Central and just across 42nd Street from it. Same architects. A $10 million project; a block-long rectangle of ten thousand tons of steel clad in redbrick and limestone. A thousand rooms; the tallest hotel in the city when it went up; lauded in guidebooks for its exquisite French decorations: "The dome and pendentives are enriched by paintings of Titania's dance from the 'Mid-summer Night's Dream.'" "Mama," asked a little girl wearing a white dress with a gray sash and black stockings in an early ad, "we will always come to this Hotel, won't we?" All the contents of the hotel were sold at public auction in 1930. By 1939, replaced by a now long-gone airlines terminal, it was already less well-remembered than many dreams. The *WPA Guide to New York City*, a definitive book, gave the Belmont only a fourteen-word look-back: "Famous for the magnificence of its bar and the cuisine of its French chefs."

Grand Central, one hundred years after its opening day, still stands. Attracting greater crowds than ever, it's a place that touches 750,000 people daily. Since 1913, it's been a place that radiates ideas that may still take another century to fully catch on. It is beloved, glowing, indispensable, and has emerged as the final, permanent structure on its site. It is a redwood amid driftwood. The Terminal's structural magnificence and the indelible mark it has made on the city are marvelously set forth by Tony Robins in the pages that follow. But for all too many years this outcome seemed questionable.

Unlike the Hotel Belmont across the street, Grand Central was not auctioned off and leveled by the Depression, but soon after, it had to outlast the postwar building boom and the reasoning that went with it: Americans of the next generation would only move around in cars and planes. Starting in the 1950s, when I was growing up, Grand Central began to seem ephemeral and maybe even unworthy of further affection. "The Grand Central Terminal," said the *New York Times* in 1954, "looks as though it were built for the ages, but people probably felt the same way about the Grand Central Depot that it replaced. Apparently, we begin to get restless about these buildings every forty years or so." In the eyes of its then co-owner, the New York Central System, Grand Central had become "a very costly luxury." The chairman of the New York Central had a solution: "World's Loftiest Tower May Rise on Site of Grand Central Terminal," announced a 1954 page-one headline in the *New York Times*. "Blueprints," said the *Times*, "call for a structure that would tower over the 102 stories and the television tower of the Empire State Building, the tallest edifice ever built by man." The design, called the Hyperboloid, a wasp-waisted, cylindrical shape supposed to resist nuclear bombs, was the dream of a brilliant young architect, I. M. Pei, who, before this project, as the Royal Institute of British Architects noted in giving him its Gold Medal in 2010, "would fly from city to city persuading mayors to apply for federal funds for slum clearance— 'healing the wounds of the city,' in Pei's telling phrase."

Some critics consider the Hyperboloid to be Pei's greatest work, and recently, at the age of ninety-two, he still regretted that it had never been built. Why wasn't it? Largely because of internal business reasons, even

1   Hotel Belmont print advertisement, 1914

2   Conceptual drawing of the Hyperboloid, designed by I.M. Pei, 1956. *Courtesy of Webb and Knapp*

though passenger railroads all over the country were already looking for imaginative ways to suppress ridership and then liquidate themselves—changing timetables, for instance, so that follow-on connecting trains left before the first train had reached the transfer point. Some voices rang out in defense of Grand Central. Two hundred and thirty-five prominent architects from all over the country drafted an appeal in *Architectural Forum*; a *Times* editorial declared that the Terminal "belongs to all America"; a commuter from South Orange, New Jersey, wrote a letter to the paper "to urge that a real crusade be started to insure the perpetuation of this landmark. Truly the main room is a magnificent one—one that is unique and a source of artistic pleasure to those whose good fortune it is to walk through it."

But this early eloquence didn't keep Grand Central's main room from almost being compressed down into a windowless basement chamber next door to the plumbing and boilers for the world's tallest edifice. Grand Central's other co-owner at the time, the New Haven Railroad, effectively doomed the idea of the Hyperboloid—"Pei's dream," as it's now called—by putting forth a more modest plan to obliterate the station with something un-grand but cheaper to build: a conventional, fifty-story office tower. No crusade sprang forward on behalf of New Yorkers' good fortune. The existing city wasn't throwing aside the next generation; at this point the new one was blocking its own path.

Unprecedentedly, that wasn't the end of the story. The cautious 1950s, the decade of the "lonely crowd" when people conformed to get ahead, was also the decade when New Yorkers started to shake off their restlessness with the older parts of town. O. Henry's wisecrack about the city, that "it'll be a great place if they ever finish it," got replaced by a new kind of outlook: that New York will be a great place as soon as we stop thinking that it's unfinished.

I remember the chord this struck. The city was becoming what by 1958 the Times, in a page-one story, was calling "a battleground of opposing philosophies of what American cities of the future should be like." There was a 1950s plan to replace Carnegie Hall with a bright red, forty-four-story office tower. But, people asked, why a new building just there? Carnegie Hall

had the sweetest, purest acoustics of any auditorium in the country. In my own neighborhood, Greenwich Village, there was a 1950s plan to run a 120-foot-wide highway through the middle of Washington Square Park as a way of connecting Fifth Avenue to a swanky new address on the south side of the park—Fifth Avenue South (West Broadway renamed)—and then down to an intersection with a Robert Moses–planned elevated river-to-river expressway along Broome Street. But—why a new road just there? Washington Square was everyone's favorite little park, celebrated by one 1950s writer as "the kindest enclave I know, an island of no pressure," and the new highway, it was said, "would turn it into a mere grassy roadside plot." There was a plan in 1960 to build a 240-foot-long, two-story, one-thousand-seat café, the Huntington Hartford Pavilion, in the southeast corner of Central Park, a millionaire's gift to the city that would have cost taxpayers nothing. But—why a café just there? Central Park was everyone's favorite big park, where every tree and square foot of grass had been sought out and committed to memory by one generation after the next for a century.

In the end, Carnegie Hall was saved; the city purchased it. Ten thousand Villagers wrote postcards to the mayor protesting the new road, and Washington Square was permanently closed to traffic. After six years of legal battles over the Hartford Pavilion, the almost million-dollar gift was brusquely declined by a new parks commissioner: "We just have to be resolute about some things. One, two, three—bang!"

The railroads had further shocks for New York. The New York Central and the New Haven, joining forces, put up a fifty-eight-story office tower in the Brutalist style next to Grand Central—the MetLife Building (originally the Pan Am Building). When it opened in 1963, it was the largest commercial building in the world. More of a skyblocker than a skyscraper, with massive, precast concrete walls of an unvarying gray that sealed off views up and down Park Avenue and along 44th Street, it set off a kind of restlessness in reverse: For the first time, New Yorkers hated buildings on sight and hoped to outlast them. "Gigantically second-rate," said the *Times*.

Across town that same year, the Pennsylvania Railroad began demolishing Grand Central's sister station,

Pennsylvania Station, completed in 1910, sinking it beneath a new Madison Square Garden and a twenty-nine-story office building. The absence of extravagant, exuberant Penn Station continues to haunt; half a century later the site remains a lingering place of deprivation in the city. Gaudier than Grand Central, the old Penn Station was the unlikely juxtaposition of two self-confident, aristocratic European moments separated by 1,600 years: Half of it surrounded you and soared over you as the oversize recreation of a vast, third-century Roman public bath, and in the other half you walked under high steel-and-glass domes and arches reminiscent of London's nineteenth-century Crystal Palace. With the loss of Penn Station, as one journalist said, "the bloom was definitely off the new."

The spirit that was growing in New York, the historic preservation movement, led to the city setting up a Landmarks Preservation Commission that since 1965 has permanently protected about 28,000 buildings at least thirty years old, including Grand Central. "Historic" sounds backward-looking, but the Commission's most significant responsibility is to safeguard the future. It sends forward the best achievements of our age and those of earlier ones—parks, a great concert hall, a superb train station—so they can enrich and transform the lives of people we'll never meet.

What is it that Grand Central, in particular, does for people? It's a question I've been trying to get to the heart of during several decades of writing about the city. In the 1970s, I noticed that "when you come up out of the subway and along a low passageway and then into the huge Main Concourse with the painting of the night sky in cerulean blue high above it, your breath stops for an instant. It's like having been preoccupied with your own affairs and suddenly remembering the vast and populous and beautiful world around you." After that I made a point of walking through Grand Central at lunchtime, since it was a couple of blocks from where I worked. By the 1990s, I realized that when you enter a room like the Main Concourse with a ceiling fifteen stories high, it feels like a weight has been lifted from your shoulders. As you move forward, you grab a chance to look down on what's going on, as well as what's going on straight ahead. Then you see that the same thing is happening to everyone else, because hundreds of people coming from all directions are moving through the room but not bumping into one another. It is a room that promotes the cooperation the city is built on.

One reason the Terminal has such an extraordinary effect is because its floors and walls have been designed to incorporate the needs of millions of travelers. It was the goal of the architects to eliminate confusion from arrivals and departures, and to that end they thought the smoothest patterns for mass movement would be if people could, like a stream, flow through the Terminal on ramps rather than cascade down staircases, like a waterfall. So, though ramps take up far more space than stairs, much of the station is staircase-free. "If a child can toddle at all," as the *Times* said a century ago, "it can toddle comfortably from a train to Forty-second Street." Because this hydraulic principle of crowd flow hadn't been in common use since the Roman Colosseum was built almost two thousand years before, temporary ramps of various heights were installed during construction "and the effect on the unconscious public was watched and noted with care." Similarly, "millions of eyes and every variety of deficient sight had their weight in deciding just what size and what shape letters to use over the train gates."

The essence of this, the shining message that Grand Central broadcasts to humanity, is that each moment can be refreshing, fulfilling, inspirational, worthwhile; that even getting to work and going home is something that can add to life's rewards and be looked forward to.

For a quarter of a century after the Hyperboloid threatened Grand Central's existence, it wasn't clear whether the Terminal could survive. Even after the station had been designated a city landmark in 1967, it took fighting a lawsuit, challenging the constitutionality of landmarking, in court after court; and raising and sustaining the real crusade of citizens that had been called for in 1954; and quiet intervention by Jacqueline Kennedy Onassis, who wrote the mayor, "Is it not cruel to let our city die by degrees?" Finally, a landmark 1978 decision by the United States Supreme Court made Grand Central's permanence a certainty. That was followed by a twenty-year campaign by Grand Central's new public owner, the Metropolitan Transportation Authority, to clean and restore the Terminal to its original grandeur. It was a labor that, under the passionate leadership of Peter E. Stangl, Metro-North's first president, meant taking on a thousand separate tasks, such as dismantling a giant advertising sign that had covered the east windows of the Concourse since 1950; and removing two inches of dust and black mastic that had been covering the skylights ever since World War II (legend has it that they were originally darkened so that enemy planes couldn't see the station); and dissolving decades of grime that had blackened the amber walls and the golden stars in the ceiling's nighttime sky.

Are the first hundred years the hardest, or are the second? An exact count doesn't exist, but it's estimated that of the approximately one million buildings in New York City, perhaps twenty-two thousand are one hundred years old. Only about nine hundred buildings have made it as far as two hundred. But Grand Central, in its centennial year, is just coming of age. The Terminal is reaching out to its neighborhood, adding entrances to the north that no one had thought of previously, and there's talk of a short greenway to the south that would tie it more closely to midtown Manhattan's other surviving early twentieth-century palace, the gleaming, white marble main branch of the New York Public Library. With one hundred carefully selected shops and restaurants,

3   Peter E. Stangl Chairman and Chief Executive Officer, MTA and the first President and General Manager of Metro-North Commuter Railroad Company receives an award from Jacqueline Kennedy Onassis, 1993. *Photograph by Frank English*

including one of the country's largest Apple stores, and the hundred-year-old Oyster Bar, as well as a specialty food market renowned for pastries, fresh seafood, and dozens of cheeses, Grand Central has become one of the world's most popular tourist attractions, getting more visitors than either Disney World or Disneyland and almost as many as Niagara Falls.

When you love a building, you come up with very different ideas for it than if you hate it. Case in point: Vanderbilt Hall, a towering, ballroom-size space adjacent to the Main Concourse, and originally the Terminal's Main Waiting Room. In 1960, the New York Central hoped to hasten the Terminal's demolition by trivializing this room, inserting Grand Central Bowl, a three-story bowling alley, into the top forty-seven feet between floor and ceiling. The bottom eleven feet, cramped and harshly lighted, would still have been available for travelers. The city vetoed the idea.

The latest thoughts about Vanderbilt Hall come from Metro-North, the railroad Grand Central now serves. Metro-North is the Terminal's current landlord, although it prefers to call itself the building's "steward." Information-technology visionaries consider the hugeness of Vanderbilt Hall a plus, and possibly a unique opportunity to present, on screens and with lights and audio, an ever-changing display of digitized images that could, among other things, show people real-time views from nearby and far away: trains twisting along the Hudson River next to the forests of the Hudson Highlands; or crowds in other great train stations, like St. Pancras Station, in London, or Chatrapati Shivaji Terminus, formerly Victoria Terminus, in Mumbai; or, more locally, shots of what the Statue of Liberty looks like at this moment.

The arc of Metro-North's story parallels that of Grand Central's comeback. It began life in 1983, as one of its own press releases acknowledges, as the "unreliable and decrepit" successor to the bankrupt commuter services of three predecessor railroads. Now the largest passenger railroad in the country, and with an on-time record approaching 100 percent, Metro-North has been redefining the shape of the New York region by extending its reach far beyond what used to be thought of as Manhattan's traditional "commuteshed." It's been suggested this could mean running trains north and northeast to two state capitals, Albany and Hartford, each more than one hundred miles from Grand Central, and to New London, at almost the eastern end of Connecticut. There's talk that Metro-North trains might swing northwest across a rebuilt Tappan Zee bridge into upstate counties on the other side of the Hudson. The railroad has already pioneered the first tristate through trains that cross the Hudson, and on football Sundays bring New York and Connecticut Giants fans to New Jersey's MetLife Stadium in the Meadowlands. In 2011, Metro-North became the first American railroad to win a Brunel Award, an international prize for excellence in railway visual design given every three years in honor of Isambard Kingdom Brunel, the brilliant nineteenth-century English engineer who, in the 1830s, founded the Great Western Railway connecting London to Birmingham, Wales, and Cornwall.

To my mind, the best thing Metro-North has done is export Grand Central's central idea that moving around is a special part of the day. Cesar Vergara, the industrial designer brought in to work on Metro-North's cheerful new red-and-silver M8 cars on the New Haven line, says he designed them "as a dissatisfied commuter. I was myself a commuter for so many years, and I didn't like it." The result is a train car that has thought about how to please you no matter where you sit. The dreaded middle seat in a row of three, the one that's not next to an aisle or a window, has become a premium seat that's now subtly and slightly wider than the seats on either side. Windows are wide and tall, almost twice the size of the ones they replace, and give you an almost movie screen–like effect of seeing deep into the world from perfect safety.

Sitting on my desk is a concrete piece of Grand Central's future—actually, it's three times harder than concrete. It's a chunk of amphibolite, sparkling, with black and gray stripes and hints of green, a half-billion-year-old rock that until recently sat undisturbed 125 feet below Park Avenue and 48th Street. The greatest change coming to Grand Central, the East Side Access project, will, in 2018, expand the station's capacity by almost half, daily bringing 124,000 Long Island Rail Road passengers who work in east midtown into Grand Central. Currently, Penn Station is the Long Island's only stop in Manhattan, and East Side Access, which has been talked about since 1966, a year before

Grand Central became a landmark, will cut Long Islanders' round-trip commutes by forty-four minutes.

To make East Side Access possible, Grand Central, which survived the high-rise onslaught three decades ago, has been extended straight downward and will be the rooftop for an adjunct station for Long Islanders that, when completed, will be a two-and-a-half-minute escalator ride below a new underground concourse. It was the only way to get safely beneath a variety of subway lines, building foundations, and Grand Central's own sub-sub-basement and buried double-decker train yard. For several years, two 400-foot-long tunnel-boring machines moving four feet forward in an hour (a speed of less than 1/1000ths of a mile per hour) ground away at bedrock. In doing so, they and TBMs excavating similar tunnels for other long-awaited projects—including a new water tunnel, the Second Avenue Subway, and an extension of the 7 line—have been exposing the city's oldest story, the history of what's far beneath our feet. It was understood to a considerable extent in pre-TBM days, but now "we've got it nailed down, lock, stock and barrel," one MTA geologist says.

It's a sub-landscape even less explored than the ocean depths, and it's had a violent past. Manhattan schist, the most commonly encountered subsurface rock in midtown, was originally the mud and sand on the bottom of the Iapetus Ocean; in Greek mythology, Iapetus was the father of Atlas, after whom the modern Atlantic Ocean is named. The Iapetus was formed three-quarters of a billion years ago when Rodinia, the fifth of seven ancient supercontinents, broke apart. Several hundred million years later, as continents reassembled and the Iapetus shrank, the ocean floor, deformed by high heat and intense pressure, became schist. At the same time, eruptions of magma from the earth's molten mantle thirty miles below the surface began forming chains of off-coast volcanic islands, something like Japan. When they, too, eventually collided with the continent of proto–North America, this lava underwent its own metamorphosis and became amphibolite. Amphibolite, schist, and other rocks have since then been squeezed, contorted, and folded into long frozen waves that under Manhattan form a giant, tilted, sheared-off A. The ceiling of Grand Central's Main Concourse has celebrated the heavens for a century. East Side Access could give New Yorkers a

look at something equally extraordinary.

Guessing how people will travel in the future is unreliable; the flying cars and personal hovercrafts and jetpacks that seemed around the corner fifty years ago have yet to appear. Nevertheless, it seems likely that steel wheels on rails—trains—will still be with us one hundred years from now, if only because they can go more than two hundred miles an hour, and at some point the price of oil could restrict travel by cars and planes. Although current plans for higher train speeds between Washington, New York, and Boston are limited to raising the speed limit to 165 miles an hour on thirty miles of track in New Jersey, my hunch is that someday—around 2050—someone will dig a high-speed rail tunnel under Manhattan deeper than East Side Access, and from Grand Central you'll get to Washington or Boston in just over an hour.

In the much nearer future, two "little Grand Centrals," as they've been called, will open in lower Manhattan, near the rebuilt World Trade Center. Both are designed to be places to linger in, not just pass through; both will bring daylight down to underground concourses; both come from prominent European architects celebrated for soaring train stations. From the outside, the white-steel-and-glass ribs of Santiago Calatrava's World Trade Center Transportation Hub look like the wings of a dove of peace, and on the inside form a lofty vault that, one admirer says, builds spectacle into daily life.

At Sir Nicholas Grimshaw's Fulton Street Transit Center, on the corner of Broadway and Fulton, daylight enters from a glass oculus sixty feet above the Main Concourse and is reflected off a cone of perforated and mirrored metal panels. "Grand Central has pictures of stars," says one of the construction team. "At night we'll have real stars." The Fulton Street center creates an orderly path linking what had been a tangle of eight subway lines, and incorporates a restored landmark building thirty-five years older than Grand Central. It's partly a post-9/11 project whose purpose is to celebrate a neighborhood that had been struggling to find its feet. But it's also a project, as one planner says, "to do something that needed doing on September 10, 2011. By Grand Central-izing downtown we can finally make moving through that part of town something to look forward to."

1
GRAND CENTRAL BEFORE THE TERMINAL

Grand Central Terminal today sits astride Park Avenue at 42nd Street in all its restored splendor—elegant triple-arched facade, massive sculpture of ancient Roman gods, and fourteen-foot-tall Tiffany clock—attracting visitors by the thousands, every hour. The hustle and energy of its daily drama as an urban crossroads are matched only by the complexity and precision of its inner workings as a transit hub. At the opening of its second century, the Terminal dominates midtown Manhattan. It is grand, it is central, and it is one of the city's great wonders.

Grand Central still plays a vital role in the city's transportation network. To think of the Terminal solely as a train station, however, is to miss its significance for New York over the past hundred years. At the beginning of the twentieth century, its development helped create midtown Manhattan—above ground, with the brand-new gilded corridor of Park Avenue and its surrounding hotels and office buildings, but also below ground, with miles of tracks and tunnels as well as turbines generating power for the buildings overhead. At the end of the twentieth century, the Terminal's rescue and restoration, with the imprimatur of the United States Supreme Court, helped secure the legitimacy of New York's landmarks law, and led a three-decades-long recovery of the city's great monuments. Always more than just a transit hub, imagined by its planners as a new civic center for the metropolis, Grand Central has functioned as an unofficial town square, home

to performances and exhibitions, patriotic gatherings and technological displays, New Year's Eve celebrations, memorials and prayers. Over time, besides ticket counters and waiting rooms, it has housed a theater and an art gallery, tennis courts and a USO lounge, stores and restaurants, and even a network television studio.

The current Terminal stands on the site of a series of buildings—a Depot, an Annex, and a Station—that have all borne the name Grand Central. When the Commodore—Cornelius Vanderbilt, founder of the vast Vanderbilt fortune—opened Grand Central Depot in 1871, its elegant design and advanced construction awed New Yorkers as much as would the future Terminal. Vanderbilt's complex claimed the title of largest train station in the country. Even so, within fifteen years, increasing demand would oblige the Commodore's successors to double the Depot's capacity with a new Annex to the east—an expansion that effectively closed off Park Avenue north of 42nd Street. Within another fifteen years, overwhelmed by still greater traffic, the Depot would give way to a new Grand Central Station, double the size of the original. Only then would planning begin for today's Terminal.

1 In 1869, even as canals and railroads crisscrossed New York State, the railway had already overtaken the slower transport of an earlier era. *Courtesy of New York State Library*

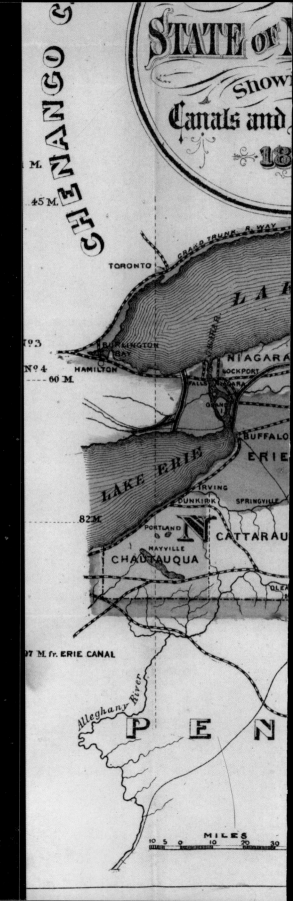

The Commodore's Grand Central Depot

"People who come to New York should enter a palace on the end of their ride, and not a shed. The stranger who visits us for business or pleasure should be impressed by the magnificence of the great city upon his very entrance within its limits. So we endorse Mr. Vanderbilt's proposed depot on 41st street. Let it be worthy of him and of the metropolis."

—*REAL ESTATE RECORD AND BUILDERS GUIDE*, JUNE 5, 1869

New York, one of the world's great port cities, relied from earliest times on water routes—harbor, rivers, and a system of canals—for its growing prosperity. But rail travel would eventually supplant water and transform the country's development. That transition was dominated in New York by Cornelius Vanderbilt—the "Commodore"—founder of one of the country's great shipping fortunes, as well as a dynasty whose name still conjures visions of vast wealth. In the 1860s, at what others might have considered retirement age, Vanderbilt bought up the city's two fledgling rail lines, the New York and Harlem Railroad and the Hudson River Railroad, and merged them with the upstate New York Central Railroad, consolidating control of rail transport into and out of the city. Because New York had banned steam engines south of 42nd Street, Vanderbilt closed down existing depots farther south and built a new 42nd Street "Grand Central Depot"—on the site of a preexisting but much smaller Harlem Railroad depot—to serve three separate lines: the New York Central and Hudson River Railroad, the New York and Harlem Railroad, and the New York, New Haven, and Hartford Railroad.

Vanderbilt's Depot—or Union Depot, as the press first styled the massive new complex—was as grand a building as New York had yet seen. It dwarfed such earlier, pre–Civil War monuments as City Hall, the U.S. Custom House on Wall Street, or the original St. Patrick's Cathedral on Mott Street. And it was intended to be a beautiful structure: the enabling State legislation specified that the depot "be substantially constructed of the best materials, and the front of said building on Forty-second street shall be of Philadelphia pressed brick, brown or freestone, or marble and iron, and shall be finished in the best style of architecture."

Beyond trumping the local competition, Vanderbilt aimed to emulate the great train terminals of Europe, in particular St. Pancras Station in London. England had pioneered railroad development and great railway stations, and St. Pancras—opened in 1868, just one year before the Commodore's new Depot took shape—claimed to have the world's largest single-span train shed. Vanderbilt's architect, John B. Snook, created a version of St. Pancras's shed almost as large as the original, and larger than anything on this side of the Atlantic. However, for the design of the head house—the Depot's public face—Snook turned away from the Victorian Gothic of St. Pancras, looking instead to what established New York fashion would consider "the best style of architecture": the style today called "Second Empire," as exemplified by the New Louvre in Paris. The architect of Vanderbilt's American depot draped French style over British technology.

From Waterways to Railways

"The discussion in relation to the capacity of railways to carry freight in opposition to canals, seems long ago to have been settled, and the canal interest, with one accord, seems to have surrendered the field to the railway."

—*AMERICAN RAILWAY TIMES*, DECEMBER 4, 1858

2   Erie Canal at Auriesville, New York. By 1890, passengers looked to the Erie Canal for recreational outings—and took the train to get there. *Courtesy of the Canal Society of New York State*

The Commodore and His Architect

"Mr. John B. Snook, a well-known architect of New York, died there a few days ago…. He [had] gained a reputation for integrity and thoroughness, which brought him friends and employment, while his work won him the respect of architects, even after professional ideas in regard to design had changed materially from those current when he began his career. His most important building was, probably, the Grand Central Railway Station."

—*AMERICAN ARCHITECT AND BUILDING NEWS*, NOVEMBER 9, 1901

3 Portrait Cornelius Vanderbilt. *Courtesy of the Library of Congress, Bain Collection*

4 An 1846 portrait of architect John B. Snook, who designed A. T. Stewart's "Marble Palace," New York's first department store and one of the city's most imposing new buildings. A quarter of a century later he designed New York's first grand train depot, again one of the city's most impressive pieces of architecture. *Collection of the New-York Historical Society*

5 Vanderbilt's home at 10 Washington Place. Despite his millions, the Commodore lived in modest surroundings, leaving his descendants to line Fifth Avenue with mansions and build huge country estates. *From* Frank Leslie's Illustrated Newspaper, *January 20, 1877. Courtesy of the Library of Congress*

"The citizens of New-York will be astonished in a few days, when they have an opportunity of beholding the colossal bronze statue, with allegorical accessories, erected in honor of Commodore Vanderbilt, on the summit of the western wall of the new and immense Hudson River Railroad Depot, situated on the former site of St. John's Park.... Whether we consider him as the great operator and financier or as the steamship Commodore and railway King, or as the man who gets married after the age appointed for men to die, or as the man who is the subject of a statue which, taken all in all, is without a parallel in this or any other country, we always find him the man of boldness, originality, and the most striking popular effects."

—*NEW YORK TIMES*, "ERECTION OF A COLOSSAL BRONZE STATUE," SEPTEMBER 2, 1869

6 Cornelius "Commodore" Vanderbilt, who died in 1877, didn't live to see the evolution of his Depot, but his statue—originally commissioned for his Hudson River Railroad Depot downtown—lives on at today's Terminal.

CORNELIVS·VANDERBILT

FOVNDER
OF THE
NEW YORK
CENTRAL
LINES

London Meets
Paris in New York

"The central space, [of Grand Central's train shed], 630 feet by 200, forms a monstrous car-house, to which admission is gained by the ten iron arches at the north end of the building. The height of this immense car-shed is ninety feet. The roof is formed of glass and corrugated iron, and is supported by thirty-one semi-circular trusses of iron, each measuring four feet in width by one foot in thickness. These trusses are painted in rich colors, and on the lower sections there is a good deal of gilding, while the iron sheeting extending between the arches is painted a blue tinge. The effect of the whole is perfectly gorgeous. At night the interior is lighted up by twelve chandeliers, each provided with one hundred lights and a large reflector. High up on the walls, in letters six feet high, are inscribed the names, 'C. Vanderbilt, president; W.H. Vanderbilt, treasurer.'"

—*THE RAILROAD GAZETTE*, JULY 1871

"Occupying, as it does, a site of nearly ten acres, [St. Pancras] is undoubtedly, if not from an architectural, at least from an engineering point of view, the finest terminus in the world. Its most interesting and peculiar feature is the roof. While it has the widest span of any roof in existence, the space beneath is unbroken by ties or braces, common to all others."

—*SCIENTIFIC AMERICAN*, DECEMBER 1869

"The sweeping lines of their gigantic curves fill the mind with the sense of harmony and repose. Are we to deny to such structures the term 'true architecture?'"

—*AMERICAN ARCHITECT AND BUILDING NEWS*, DESCRIBING THE IRON ROOFS OF ST. PANCRAS AND GRAND CENTRAL, DECEMBER 20, 1884

7   New York: The Grand Central Depot train shed.

8   London: St. Pancras train shed.
The pointed-arch roof at St. Pancras reflected the Victorian Gothic of the exterior. Snook, instead, designed a round, segmental arch for the roof of the Depot. *Photograph © Alan Copson/Robert Itarding World Imagery/Corbis*

9

"The mansard roof, which, since its introduction by Lienau and Marcotte on the house built by Madame Shiff in New York some twenty years ago, has dominated the superstructures of this whole land as completely as the Greek Temple did at one time."

—ADDRESS ON THE HISTORY OF AMERICAN ARCHITECTURE AT THE TENTH ANNUAL CONVENTION OF THE AMERICAN INSTITUTE OF ARCHITECTS, OCTOBER 1876

10

9 Paris: the New Louvre, completed in 1857 for Napoleon III. *Photograph by Eric Pouhier*

10 New York: Grand Central Depot, completed in 1871 for Commodore Vanderbilt. The French Renaissance style of the New Louvre—and especially the characteristic tall mansard roof—became the hallmark of fashionable American architecture following the Civil War. New York architects adopted the style for such contemporaries of the Depot as the new post office in City Hall Park, office buildings and banks, hotels and mansions, as well as proposals for the new State Capitol in Albany.

"A Triumph of Mechanical Ingenuity"

"The enormous building now being constructed for a Union Depot of the Hudson, New Haven, and Harlem railroads, is one of those wonders of mechanical design and ingenuity well worthy of attention to all those interested in such matters. The work is proceeding with such extraordinary speed that, to any one who allows the interval of only a week to elapse between his visits, the progress appears almost like the work of enchantment."

—*REAL ESTATE RECORD AND BUILDERS GUIDE,* NOVEMBER 5, 1870

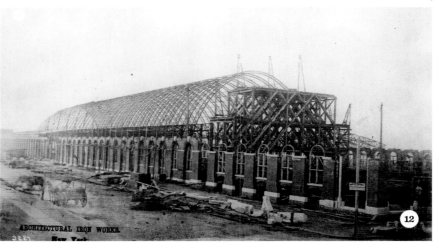

"The scaffolding alone, erected for putting these ponderous masses of iron in place, is worth a visit; and the roof, when completed, will be a triumph of mechanical ingenuity."

—*REAL ESTATE RECORD AND BUILDERS GUIDE,* SEPTEMBER 17, 1870

"The train-house portion of this great building was erected with extraordinary rapidity, by means of a travelling stage, upon which the arched girder trusses were successively built and placed in position."

—*AMERICAN ARCHITECT AND BUILDING NEWS,* NOVEMBER 29, 1884

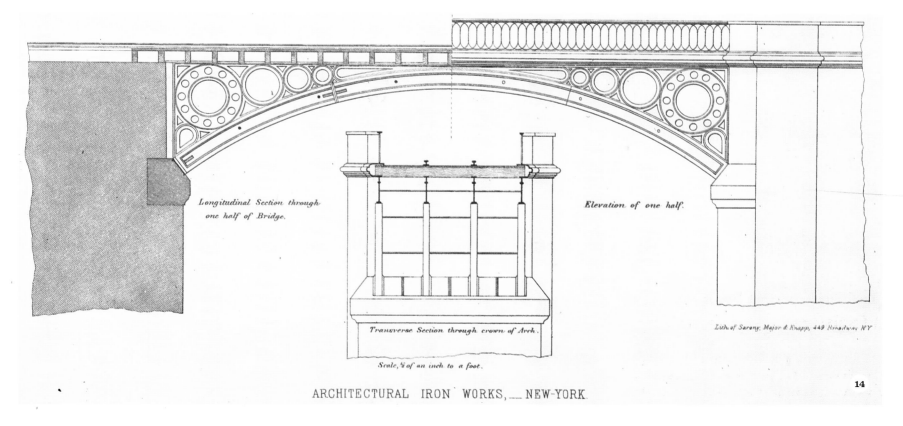

Longitudinal Section through one half of Bridge.

Elevation of one half.

Transverse Section through crown of Arch.

Scale, ⅛ of an inch to a foot.

Lith of Sarony, Major & Knapp, 449 Broadway NY.

ARCHITECTURAL IRON WORKS, — NEW-YORK.

14

"Among the many unexampled improvements in this new enterprise are the stone platforms, the steam heating arrangements, gates, and other contrivances for the convenience, safety and comfort of travelers…. It will be the largest and most complete depot, in every particular, in the world."

—*NEW YORK TIMES*, DECEMBER 8, 1870

11 The Depot, rear facade. The train shed is visible inside.

12 The train shed under construction by Architectural Iron Works, one of New York's major foundries, famous for cast-iron facades in lower Manhattan.

13 Elaborate ornamental iron detail by Architectural Iron Works, elevating the train shed's design beyond the purely utilitarian, 1871.

14 Design for a single track bridge, Architectural Iron Works catalog, 1865.

15 'The interior of the shed, 1875.

15

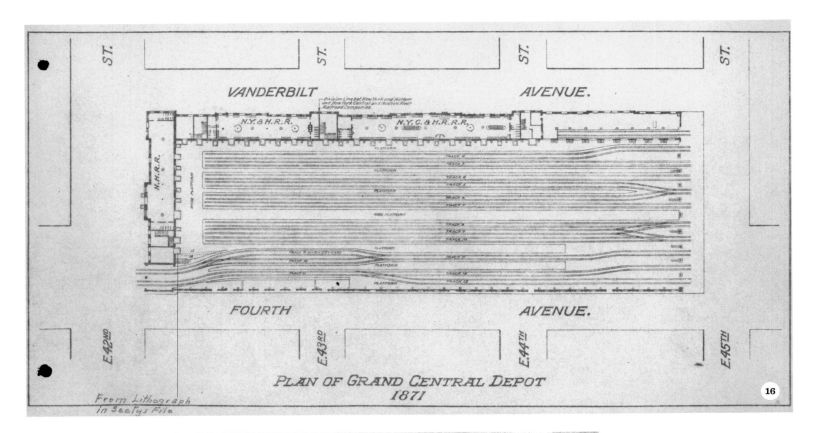

VANDERBILT AVENUE.

ST. ST. ST. ST.

Division Line bet. New York and Harlem
and New York Central and Hudson River
Railroad Companies.

N.Y. & H.R.R. N.Y.C. & H.R.R.R.

N.H.R.R.

FOURTH AVENUE.

E.42ND E.43RD E.44TH E.45TH

PLAN OF GRAND CENTRAL DEPOT
1871

From Lithograph
in Seelys File

16

N.Y. CENTRAL & HUDSON R.R.

ARCHITECTURAL IRON WORKS.
New York.

17

16 The ground plan of Grand Central Depot. The L-shaped head house framed the 42nd Street and Vanderbilt Avenue sides of the complex, with three waiting rooms for three separate railroads: the New Haven on 42nd Street, and the Harlem and Hudson lines along Vanderbilt Avenue.

17 Grand Central Depot, c. 1870. The head house's three towers along 42nd Street represent the three separate stations within Grand Central Depot serving three lines. The 42nd Street wing, to the right, housed waiting rooms and ticket offices for the New York and New Haven line, as well as such passenger amenities as restrooms, restaurants, and newsstands. The Vanderbilt Avenue wing, to the left, included waiting rooms for the other two lines, as well as baggage rooms. Railway company offices occupied the upper two stories. A major city monument, the Depot quickly became a popular tourist attraction.

18

"A Magnificent Ornament to the City"

"This is decidedly the largest and handsomest depot in the world. Its exterior is imposing, and its immense size and regularity gives it a marked magnitude in a city where there is so much architectural discord…. It is well worth the time for a stranger in our city to pay a visit to this rightly named 'Grand Depot of the World.'"

—*MILLER'S NEW YORK AS IT IS, OR STRANGER'S GUIDE-BOOK TO THE CITIES OF NEW YORK, BROOKLYN, AND ADJACENT PLACES, C. 1880*

"Among all our large commercial buildings, the railroad depots are those of which New Yorkers have least cause to be proud…. But at last a building has been erected, where space for business, order and discipline in arrangement, ample ingress and egress, and substantial elegance of interior and exterior, are provided. This is the new Union depot…. The travelling public will appreciate the convenience of the new terminus, and one of our railway presidents will have got rid, as far as he is concerned, of a lasting reproach to New York."

—*SCIENTIFIC AMERICAN*, JULY 15, 1871

18 Horse-drawn transportation connecting the Depot with the city, which was still concentrated to the south.

"The New Underground Railway on Fourth Avenue"

"The Forty-second street depot is simply an enormous nuisance where it stands, a source of great public danger; it cuts the city into two parts, and makes traffic from east to west above Forty-second street a matter of imminent peril to life and limb. And as the Commodore has shown no disposition whatever to serve the public, there is no mercy to be shown to him when the question of public convenience impends. All good citizens, from this time forth, will insist that Commodore Vanderbilt must clear off this island."

—*REAL ESTATE RECORD AND BUILDERS GUIDE*, FEBRUARY 10, 1872

"A portion of the new Underground Railway, on Fourth avenue, has just been opened for traffic, namely, from the Grand Central Depot at 42nd street, northerly to 98th street, over two miles. All the trains of the Harlem, Hudson River, and New Haven Companies now run underground, and their withdrawal from the surface of Fourth avenue gives great satisfaction to the inhabitants residing on the line. The vibration produced by the passage of trains is scarcely noticeable in the adjoining houses. The avenue surface above the railway tunnels is now being repaved, and will soon present a most beautiful, attractive appearance. A stranger in passing through this portion of the avenue would be surprised if told that, directly under his feet, the trains of three great railways were flying along at lightning speed."

—*SCIENTIFIC AMERICAN*, JUNE 5, 1875

19

"It will be a crying outrage indeed if the railroads centring at Vanderbilt's depot on Forty-second street, are permitted in defiance of public sentiment to continue the course they have followed within the past three months, and be permitted to kill and maim citizens day after day by running trains of cars on open and unguarded tracks at all hours."

—*EVENING TELEGRAM*, MARCH 14, 1872

FRANK LESLIE'S ILLUSTRATED NEWSPAPER. [FEBRUARY 15, 187

19 Fourth Avenue (later renamed Park Avenue) at 52nd and 53rd streets, 1865. Vanderbilt's Depot drew extravagant praise from the press. No sooner had the Depot opened, however, then the press discovered that the tracks of the new train yard completely overwhelmed "the Fourth Avenue." *Courtesy of the New-York Historical Society*

20 Though some of the tracks along Fourth Avenue had been lowered below grade even before construction of Vanderbilt's Depot, the vast open train yard just to its north presented new problems. The public outcry quickly forced Vanderbilt to lower the tracks into an open cut in the middle of the avenue, from 49th to 56th Street (as shown in this 1890 photo), with bridges connecting east and west for pedestrians, and a series of tunnels to the north.

21 "Beam tunnels," open at the top but spanned by a series of iron beams, enclosed the tracks from 56th to 67th Street and again from 71st to 80th Street.

22 The central portion of the beam tunnel shown here in 1909, accommodated two tracks; an additional tunnel on each side had a single track. Trains passed through fully enclosed brick tunnels from 67th to 71st Street and from 80th to 96th Street. Today the entire stretch from Grand Central Terminal to 97th Street is underground.

"Extending the Big Depot"

In the decade following the opening of the Commodore's Depot, New York grew mightily in population, commerce, and influence, and railway traffic increased accordingly. In 1883, the Brooklyn Bridge linked the still separate cities of New York and Brooklyn, prompting *Century Illustrated Magazine* to wonder: "Will New York Be the Final World Metropolis?" The pressure of growth led to the construction of an annex on the east side of the Depot, opened in 1885, which added seven tracks, on five platforms, to the Depot's existing twelve tracks. The Depot already stretched east from Vanderbilt Avenue to Fourth Avenue, but left Fourth Avenue unobstructed. Expanding farther east meant closing Fourth Avenue between 42nd and 45th streets, and creating Depew Place—named for New York Central president Chauncey Depew—as an eastern counterpart to Vanderbilt Avenue, to accommodate the redirected traffic flow.

The Commodore did not live to see the expansion of his Depot. Power devolved to his eldest son, William H. Vanderbilt, who took over the reins of the New York Central and guided the growth of the railroad, greatly increasing the scope of his father's empire. It was also William who first led the opulent lifestyle associated with the Vanderbilt name.

"The general public little appreciates the work imposed upon railroad officials in handling a passenger traffic that has grown beyond the facilities of the station where it is received. Travellers ... will rejoice ... along with the station and train men of the New-York Central Railroad, at the prospect of an addition to the Grand Central Depot which will practically double the facilities and capacity of the present building."
—*NEW-YORK TRIBUNE*, EDITORIAL, FEBRUARY 19, 1884

"Plans have been filed for a new passenger-depot ... similar to that of the Grand Central Depot, the front being made of brick and cast-iron, with stone trimmings. The estimated cost is $200,000."
—*AMERICAN ARCHITECT AND BUILDING NEWS*, NOVEMBER 29, 1884

R-2683-2-17-07
C C YARD IMP. CONCOURSE IN ANNEX. LOOKING W.

N. Y. RECORDER SOUVENIR.

№ 62193

VANDERBILT HOUSES, FIFTH AVENUE.

25

26

"From the Spring of 1877 to the Fall of 1881—barely five years—William H. Vanderbilt was wholly in charge of the great railroads which his father had bequeathed to him.... In three years William H. Vanderbilt had doubled the colossal fortune left him by his father, and had become, beyond all comparison, the richest man in the world."
—W. A. CROFFUT, "WILLIAM H. VANDERBILT," *FRANK LESLIE'S POPULAR MONTHLY*, 1886

"Had his father been a man of only moderate wealth, his son would undoubtedly have burst away from the repressive control and influence which surrounded him. But no man could afford to throw away his chances of becoming heir to $100,000,000, and hence prudence kept him for so many good years of his life in the passive attitude of a prince, one day destined for a throne, but excluded by the ruling sovereign from any participation in the control of affairs. But at last the hour of recognition came."
—LAURA CARTER HOLLOWAY, *FAMOUS AMERICAN FORTUNES AND THE MEN WHO HAVE MADE THEM*, 1884

"William H. Vanderbilt has lately completed, on Fifth Avenue, two splendid palaces, studiously modest without, as beseems his Dutch ancestry, but adorned within by the most rare and expensive works of art of every description.... Mrs. Vanderbilt, a most amiable, lovely and refined lady, is one of the queens of society, and to give her a palace worthy of her queenly state, the Vanderbilt mansions have been erected, and Art has been benefited by an almost unlimited patronage."
—STEPHEN FISKE, *OFF-HAND PORTRAITS OF PROMINENT NEW YORKERS*, 1884

23 The 1885 Annex connecting to the Third Avenue Elevated station at its Park Avenue spur, looking northeast, 1907. The Annex survived the 1891–1901 reconstruction of the Depot, succumbing only to the new Grand Central Terminal after the turn of the century.

24 Annex interior, looking west into the original train shed, 1907.

25 Double houses of William H. Vanderbilt, Fifth Avenue from 51st to 52nd Street, several blocks north and west of Grand Central Depot. *Courtesy of the Picture Collection, the New York Public Library, Astor, Lenox and Tilden Foundations*

26 William Henry Vanderbilt, the Commodore's eldest son. Outliving his father by only eight years, he died in 1885, just as the Annex opened.

"The commodore's offer of the attorneyship for the Harlem Railroad, which was his first venture in railroading, was far less than the salary as minister [to Japan; a post which Depew had just accepted]. When I said this to the commodore, he remarked: 'Railroads are the career for a young man; there is nothing in politics. Don't be a damned fool.' That decided me."

—CHAUNCEY MITCHELL DEPEW, *MY MEMORIES OF EIGHTY YEARS*, 1921

27 Chauncey Depew, 1898. Hired as a lawyer for the New York and Harlem Railroad by Commodore Vanderbilt, Depew became president of the New York Central in 1885, the year the Annex opened, and served as chairman of the board from 1898 until his death in 1928. Depew's name survives at East 45th Street in the short stretch of Depew Place—originally created to accommodate the Annex—where a viaduct now carries traffic around the eastern side of Grand Central Terminal. *Courtesy of the Museum of the City of New York, Byron Co. Collection*

Expansion: Grand Central Station

The new Annex might have almost doubled the size of the Depot, but between the early 1870s and the late 1890s the city's railroad traffic quadrupled, leading to a major rebuilding of Grand Central. The three railways sharing the building badly needed more office space for their operations, and the passengers using the building needed a unified facility not broken up among the three railways. In early 1896, the rail companies announced an expansion that would all but create a new building in place of the Depot. They turned to their chief engineer, Walter Katté, and brought in architect Bradford L. Gilbert. According to a *Chicago Tribune* article in 1892, Gilbert was "famed throughout America and much of Europe as a designer of railway stations." He had designed Chicago's Illinois Central Station, completed in 1893.

Gilbert's work at Grand Central Station (as it became known) added three new stories atop the original, and replaced its now outdated Second Empire–style facades with a more fashionable, classically inspired design. Inside, the new station included significant mechanical upgrades, including elevators, steam heat, a new power station, and—a major advance—electric lighting throughout.

Gilbert proposed a dramatic, barrel-vaulted rotunda waiting room—modeled on the rotunda of his Chicago station—to replace the three separate waiting rooms of the individual railways, but delays, blamed on recalcitrance by the New Haven line, kept the interior work from going forward for several years. By that time, Gilbert had been replaced by Philadelphia architect Samuel Huckle Jr., and Katté by William Wilgus, an engineer who would soon play a major role in creating Grand Central Terminal. The waiting room was built to Huckle's design rather than Gilbert's.

"The Grand Central yard is now one of the most crowded in the country.... The number of trains here are so great that even with a considerable amelioration of the conditions, the yard movements would still be very heavy. Engines are flying around in so many directions that injuries to employees are somewhat frequent, and no financial obstacles should stand in the way of the substantial abatement of the confusion now existing."

—*RAILWAY GAZETTE*, DECEMBER 1889

Elevation of Reconstructed Grand Central Station, New York City.

"The Largest, Finest, and Most Comfortable Railroad Station in the World."

"The exterior of the building is to be altered considerably, but Mr. Gilbert's aim has been to combine the new with the old so that it will harmonize completely. The entire exterior of the plain brick walls will be covered with a Portland cement stucco, which will give the effect of a solid, rough gray background, with trimmings of white.... When completed it will be one of the finest stations in the world in all its appointments."

—*AMERICAN ENGINEER, CAR BUILDER AND RAILROAD JOURNAL*, 1897

"Though the station ... is not to be pulled down, so far as appearances will go it might just as well be, for all the old towers will be destroyed and the mansard roof taken away, and four stories of red brick and granite composition are to rise on the two stories left standing. Hardly a trace of the old building will seem to remain."

—*NEW-YORK TRIBUNE*, OCTOBER 3, 1897

28 Bradford Lee Gilbert. *From The National Cyclopædia of American Biography, Volume 14.*

29 Bradford Gilbert's preliminary plan for enlarging Grand Central Station added classically inspired elements, including temple fronts above the entrances, but retained the Depot's distinctive mansard roofs—though with angular, rather than curving, lines.

THE GENERAL WAITING-ROOM—THE LARGEST IN THE WORLD—LOOKING NORTHEAST.

"New York is at last to have a genuine 'union' station.... Instead of three cramped waiting rooms, separated from each other by brick walls, there will be one spacious, high-ceiled, properly lighted modern waiting room, wherein travelers bound eastward, westward, or northward may buy their tickets.... When the improvements are all finished, in a year or two, the Grand Central Station will probably be the largest, finest, and most comfortable railroad station in the world."

—*NEW YORK TIMES*, AUGUST 30, 1897

"Up in the air, three stories above ground, unmindful of the great incoming and outgoing traffic that never ceases from daylight till sunset and continues well into the night, heedless of all this and not interfering with it in the least, the wreckers of the old and the builders of the new Grand Central Station are steadfastly working side by side."

—*NEW-YORK TRIBUNE*, OCTOBER 3, 1897

30 Grand Central Station, expanded and updated, c. 1902. Its new domed towers, bearing enormous clocks, were flanked by eleven cast-iron eagles with wingspans of fourteen feet. Demolition of the Depot and construction of the Station proceeded simultaneously, while train service continued uninterrupted. The Annex is visible on the far right.

31 Gilbert's unrealized design for a rotunda at Grand Central Station, 1897, from *Harper's Weekly*

32 Gilbert's Rotunda at Chicago's Illinois Central Station, 1892. *Sketch Portfolio of Railway Stations*

"It was important in connection with railway-trains to keep exact time.... The condition of the matter was abnormal in numerous instances, there being no less than three hundred points where railroads, using different standards of time, crossed each other and exchanged traffic.... On the day when the new standards took effect, the clocks of about twenty thousand railway-stations and the watches of three hundred thousand railway employes [*sic*] were reset. Hundreds, perhaps thousands, of city and town clocks were altered to conform. How many individuals reset their watches it is impossible to compute, but they could certainly be reckoned by millions. Probably no such singular incident has ever before happened, or is likely to occur again."

—*SCIENTIFIC AMERICAN*, DECEMBER 20, 1884

33 Clocks at Grand Central Depot . On November 18, 1883, prompted by the railroads' need for consistent train schedules for safety's sake, cities and towns across the United States adopted standard time zones. Railroads set the standard, and large clocks featured prominently in each version of Grand Central.

34 Clocks at Grand Central Station.

35 Clock at Grand Central Terminal. *Photograph by Frank English*

COPR. DETROIT PHOTOGRAPHIC CO.

36

"The new waiting room [opening to the public today] will be larger than the three old passenger rooms put together, its dimensions being 200 by 100 feet. As it is nearly 70 feet high and finished entirely in marble and white stucco, with a glass roof, it will be much lighter and more airy than the old rooms, which were noted for their gloomy and generally dismal appearance."

—*NEW YORK TIMES*, OCTOBER 18, 1900

36 After thirty years of keeping separate waiting rooms for the three lines, the new Grand Central Station took a giant step toward integrating service by creating one large waiting room. Gilbert's successor, Samuel Huckle Jr., designed the unified waiting room, replacing Gilbert's proposed barrel-vaulted rotunda with a flat-ceilinged, classically inspired space not unlike its eventual replacement in the new Terminal. Photo c. 1904. *Courtesy of the Library of Congress, Prints and Photographs Division, Detroit Publishing Company Collection*

37 Grand Central Station train shed, c. 1902.

The Third Generation

"The Vanderbilts are house builders, and each new move of theirs in this direction is one in advance of the others. These enormous houses were the wonder and admiration of the city when first built, by their hugeness and lavish carvings of the stone employed."

—*NEW YORK TIMES*, OCTOBER 12, 1902

40 Cornelius Vanderbilt's French château at Fifth Avenue and 57th Street. The site is now occupied by the Bergdorf Goodman department store. *Courtesy of the Library of Congress, Prints and Photographs Division, Detroit Publishing Company Collection*

38 William K. Vanderbilt's French château at Fifth Avenue and 52nd Street. *Photograph by B. J. Falk. Courtesy of the Library of Congress, Prints and Photographs Division*

39, 41 William K. Vanderbilt and Cornelius Vanderbilt II. When William H. Vanderbilt became president of the New York Central, following the Commodore's death in 1877, his two sons became vice presidents. William K. controlled finances, while Cornelius II handled operations, and the two took charge after William H.'s retirement in 1883. Cornelius II died in 1899, and William K. gradually withdrew from direct control of the affairs of the railroad.

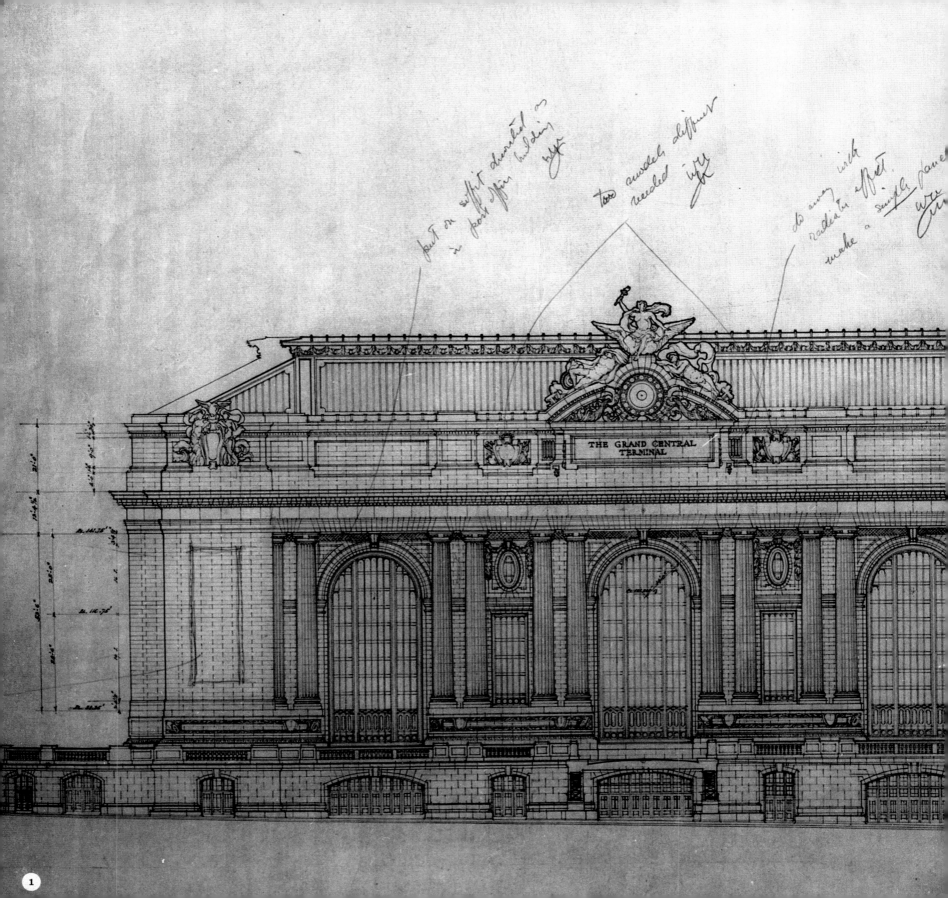

1

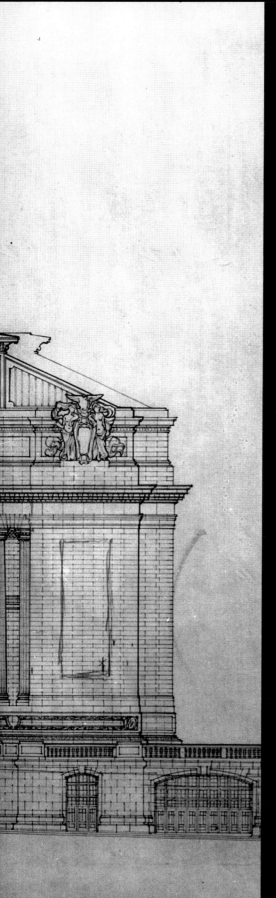

2
A TERMINAL FOR THE NEW METROPOLIS

Even with all its improvements, the reconstructed Grand Central Station remained a nineteenth-century train terminal, home to steam-powered locomotives that belched smoke and ash as they ran beneath Park Avenue, inside thirty-year-old tunnels meant to handle a fraction of the train traffic now pouring in and out of the city. Though the rebuilding of Grand Central eased the crowding in its offices and waiting rooms, changes in New York's geography, economy, and technology almost instantly rendered the Station outdated.

While in 1871 Grand Central Depot's 42nd Street location put it at the far north end of the city, by 1900 the expanded Station found itself in the center of the newly consolidated City of Greater New York. A depot with an open-air rail yard monopolizing more than a dozen blocks of real estate could exist at the city's edge, but not in the blossoming heart of a massive metropolis, just east of the mansions of newly prestigious Fifth Avenue. Also, as midtown became ever more central within the city, running steam engines through smoke-filled tunnels under Park Avenue—tunnels once welcomed as a solution to the problem of train traffic—became ever more controversial. Moreover, growth brought increased transportation needs. In 1871, Grand Central averaged 12,500 passengers daily; by 1900 that number

had risen to 50,000. Increasing demand required a major expansion, but with the existing rail yard already taking up too much midtown real estate, expanding the yard seemed impossible. Some thought it just a matter of time before Grand Central would relocate far from midtown, perhaps to Mott Haven in the Bronx, putting the Station once again at the city's periphery.

Instead, William J. Wilgus, a visionary New York Central engineer, reimagined Grand Central's structure and infrastructure by thinking vertically instead of horizontally, by harnessing new technology, and by recognizing an overlooked commodity of such enormous financial value that it could pay for the entire project. And two architectural firms—Reed & Stem and Warren & Wetmore—refashioned Grand Central's architectural identity and its place within the city by reimagining it as a grand monument at the heart of a new metropolitan civic center. The resulting complex—a huge construction project that took a decade to complete—brought the city not just a new terminal, but an entire new neighborhood.

1 Grand Central Terminal final elevation drawing, by Warren & Wetmore and Reed & Stem, with handwritten notes by Whitney Warren, c. 1910.

A Nineteenth-Century Station in a Twentieth-Century Metropolis

"While wondering at the speed with which this train approaches the station, you suddenly discover that its locomotive is running alone, and at some distance ahead of its following cars, from which it seems to have broken away. From a certain point the locomotive takes a track that runs outside the station, while from the same point the train follows another line of rails, over which it rolls of its own momentum into the great building. You have witnessed the making of 'a flying switch,' and a very neat one at that."

—*HARPER'S YOUNG PEOPLE*, MAY 23, 1893

Smoke and ash from steam engines caused two kinds of problems for Grand Central: the aesthetic problem of a smoke-filled and sooty head house, and the safety problem of running trains through smoke-filled tunnels. Early on, the railroads' determination to keep smoke out of the station interior gave rise to the flying switch, an extraordinary maneuver meant to keep locomotives out of the train shed itself. The train's engineer raced toward the station, and at the last moment uncoupled the locomotive, deflecting it onto a track leading in another direction, while the sheer momentum of the remaining cars carried them, unaided, into the shed, where the brake operator slowed them to a halt at exactly the right moment. Amazingly, this procedure caused no accidents. But no comparable procedure could keep smoke out of the Park Avenue tunnels, where conditions for travelers became unbearable.

Electric power had recently found a role in train travel. In 1900, coinciding with the internationally influential Paris Exposition Universelle, the Gare d'Orsay became the first major train station designed for electrically powered trains. Ideas for transforming Grand Central's operations by switching from steam to electricity had begun percolating as early as 1899, but it took a deadly accident to force the issue. On the morning of January 8, 1902, an incoming New Haven train came to a halt in the Park Avenue tunnel. Moments later, an incoming Harlem-line train plowed into it, killing fifteen passengers and seriously injuring another thirty-six, of whom two subsequently died. Apparently, smoke and steam had so obscured visibility in the tunnel that the engineer of the Harlem train simply couldn't see the signals. Three days later, on January 11, 1902, the *New York Times* reported that the New York Central would be switching to electric power. And the following year, after a series of hearings and meetings, an indignant State legislature ordered the railroad to give up steam by July 1, 1908.

2   Rear of Grand Central Station and yard, 1898.

2

"Indignation, Pity, and Amazement"

"When the first Grand Central Station was built it was away uptown; almost, it might be said, in the open country. But being the only station in New York city, it became the center of an active development. The great hotels, amusement places and the retail stores saw an advantage in being within easy reach of it; the famous residence and club district sprang up around it; many of the most beautiful buildings in the city were erected within a short distance of it, and thus it is that to-day Grand Central is in the very heart of the district that the visitor to New York wishes most to see, and not, as railroad stations often are, in an obscure or unattractive part of the city."

—*BANKERS' MAGAZINE*, JANUARY 1913

3 The Grand Central yard in 1891. Frank Leslie's Illustrated Newspaper. *June 6, 1891. Randall Fleischer Collection.*

4 The yard in 1908. The growing city, pushing ever farther to the north, caught up with—and quickly moved past—Grand Central Station.

5 A steam-powered locomotive heading north through the train yard, along Park Avenue between East 46th and East 50th streets, 1903.

SCENE OF WRECK 20 MINUTES AFTER OCCURRENCE DRAWN FROM PHOTOGRAPH BY CHAS. CASTEL

POLICE AND FIREMEN REMOVING THE DEAD AND INJURED FROM THE TELESCOPED CAR. **6**

"The tunnel, the dreadful smoke-filled tunnel, against which all New York has long stormed and protested, is responsible for the murderous collision of yesterday.... The engineer of the Harlem train could not see the signals in the thick atmosphere of the tunnel filled with steam and smoke. It is unlikely that anybody could have seen them. Having no warning that the train ahead of him had come to a standstill, the Harlem engineer ran as if he had a clear track, and the collision and slaughter resulted."

—*NEW YORK TIMES*, JANUARY 9, 1902

"The thousands who daily travel through the Park-ave. tunnel on railroad trains are the victims of unspeakable tortures. Let a car with doors and windows tightly closed stand in the burning sun for an hour or two until to its inmost recesses it is quivering with heat, then crowd it full of perspiring humanity, keep the doors and windows closed and drag it through several miles of hot, smoky, gas reeking tunnel, and you will have a pretty effective imitation of the Black Hole of Calcutta. And that is what thousands of people have to endure daily in the heart of the greatest city in the Western Hemisphere, and on one of the greatest, richest and most progressive railroads in the world. It is a state of affairs calculated to arouse mingled feelings of indignation, pity and amazement."

—*NEW-YORK TRIBUNE*, JULY 2, 1901 (ONE DAY AFTER THE "HOTTEST JULY 1 ON RECORD")

6   *The World*, January 9, 1902.

7   "At the Grand Central Station" cartoon,
      Life, April 17, 1902.

AT THE GRAND CENTRAL STATION. **7**

She : JIM AND I HOPE YOU'LL HAVE A PLEASANT JOURNEY, MOTHER.
Jim : YES. JUST THINK, IN SEVEN MINUTES FROM NOW YOU'LL EITHER BE SAFELY THROUGH THE TUNNEL, OR ELSE BE LYING SOMEWHERE MANGLED BEYOND RECOGNITION.

William J. Wilgus: The Chief Engineer Reimagines Grand Central

William J. Wilgus, an engineer from upstate New York, joined the New York Central in 1893, rose to be chief engineer by 1899, and in 1903 became fifth vice president, in charge of the electrification and building of Grand Central Terminal. Conflicts within the company led to his departure in 1907, before the new Terminal's completion, but it was Wilgus who devised the brilliant plan that would create a new Grand Central for the new metropolis in the new century.

Wilgus proposed, planned, and supervised the electrification of all trains entering and leaving the Terminal—a new technology recently adopted in Paris at the Gare d'Orsay and being developed in New York for the Pennsylvania Railroad and the new subway. Replacing steam locomotives with electric instantly solved the problem of smoke and steam in the Park Avenue tunnels, making it possible to enclose the tunnels completely.

But electrification did more than that: it made possible the expansion of Grand Central's train yard many times over, while at the same time removing it altogether from Park Avenue. This was accomplished by sinking the entire yard completely underground, which also recaptured a sizable chunk of midtown Manhattan for the city. Moreover, if Wilgus could sink one train yard underground, why not sink a second one? The conflicting schedules and needs of long-distance and commuter trains, long an irritant at the station, disappeared with his proposal for a two-level underground train yard: the upper level for long-distance trains, the lower level reserved for commuter lines.

With electrification, locomotives could glide, smokeless, alongside the underground platforms, rendering the flying switch unnecessary. But turning trains and locomotives around in a terminal—at the end of the line—made for complicated maneuvering, especially for heavily trafficked commuter lines. Wilgus solved that problem by creating a system of looping tracks, which enabled trains to arrive at the station, discharge passengers, continue around on the loop, and head back out.

Finally, Wilgus conceived the means for paying for such an enormous project. Demolishing some two hundred buildings, excavating the equivalent of sixteen city blocks, constructing two underground rail yards, building the infrastructure necessary to create the required electric power, and constructing a brand-new and much larger terminal building, all came at an enormous price—initial estimates came in at $43 million, in 1903 dollars. But where others saw an insurmountable financial obstacle, Wilgus saw an unrivaled financial opportunity. The New York Central owned or would acquire all those city blocks, together with the intangible asset that Wilgus called "air rights": the right to build above them. Sixteen city blocks, formerly at the outskirts of town but now in the heart of Manhattan, would be available for intensive real estate development. Properly managed, that development would generate vast amounts of capital and pay for the entire enterprise.

WILLIAM H. NEWMAN
President, June 3, 1901—February 1, 1909

"Dear Sir: I take pleasure in sending to you herewith a portfolio of suggested preliminary plans for a proposed Grand Central Terminal to be constructed in conjunction with the depression of our yard.... These suggested plans, in addition to offering attractive hotel, office, restaurant, store and railroad space ... will probably make it the most attractive locality in New York City and gain for us the approval of the general public and the municipal authorities."

—LETTER FROM "W. J. WILGUS, FIFTH VICE PRESIDENT," TO "MR. W. H. NEWMAN, PRESIDENT," MARCH 19, 1903

8   William J. Wilgus. *The Technical World*, February 1905.

9   William H. Newman, President, New York Central.

"This Pioneer Electric Installation"

"Paris is a civilized city.... A piece of ground on the river front happened to come into the market, and electrical development, allowing of electrical traction, synchronized with this opportunity. The result is that the railway has built a station which is one of the architectural ornaments of Paris, on the Quai d'Orsay.... Would it not be within the financial power of the 'Vanderbilt system' to send a competent electrical engineer out to Paris to find out just how this feat has been performed which the system keeps on repeating is beyond the power of man?"

—*NEW YORK TIMES*, NOVEMBER 7, 1901

10 Gare d'Orsay, Paris, the first station built specifically for electrically powered trains running partially underground, opened in the summer of 1900, even as Wilgus developed plans for the electrification of the New York Central. *Photo Credit: © LL/Roger-Violet/The Image Works*

11 With Wilgus himself at the controls, an electrically powered train made a ceremonial "first run" from Highbridge in upper Manhattan to Grand Central on September 30, 1906.

"With the exception of the jolting up of the passengers in the run from Fifty-sixth to Fifty-second Street over a 'dead' track and the old style interlocking switches, the trip was made with the usual speed and a great deal more comfort than the ordinary method of railroad traffic affords. The party, made up of electrical engineers from all over the country and many railroad men ... gathered at Highbridge to enter the train, which was made up of two private cars and five Pullman coaches."

—*NEW YORK TIMES*, OCTOBER 1, 1906

"The great work undertaken and practically completed by you, of changing the power within the so-called electric zone and the reconstruction of the Grand Central Station, was the most stupendous work of engineering I have ever known; and it has gone forward practically without a halt, certainly without a failure in any essential feature.... In my experience of nearly forty years I have known of no other engineer whom I feel could have accomplished what you have."

—LETTER TO WILGUS ON HIS RESIGNATION, FROM NEW YORK CENTRAL VICE PRESIDENT BROWN, JULY 5, 1907

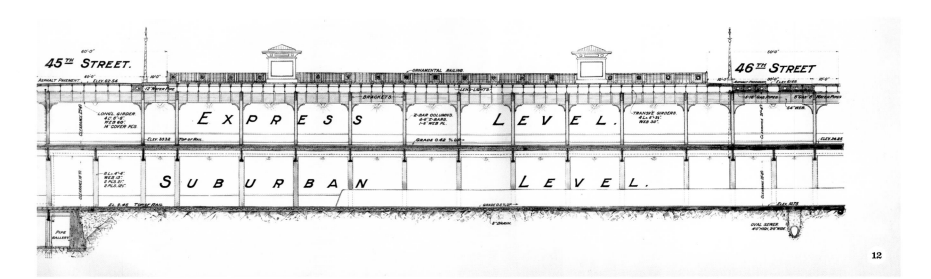

12

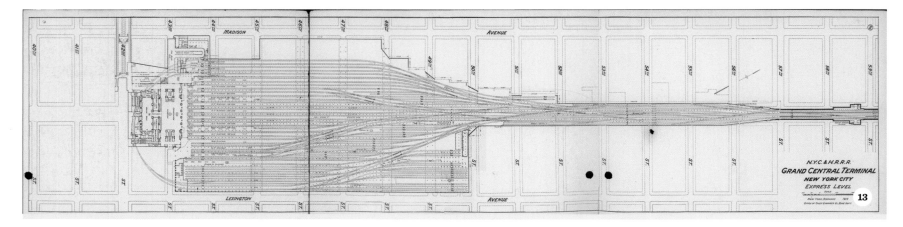

13

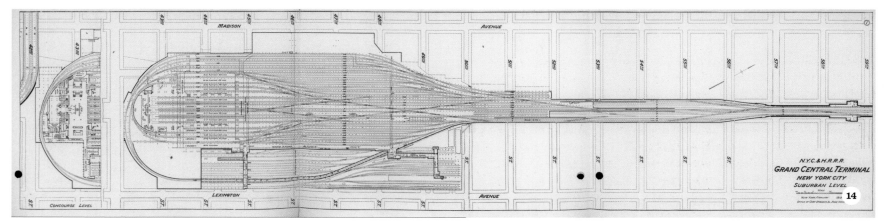

14

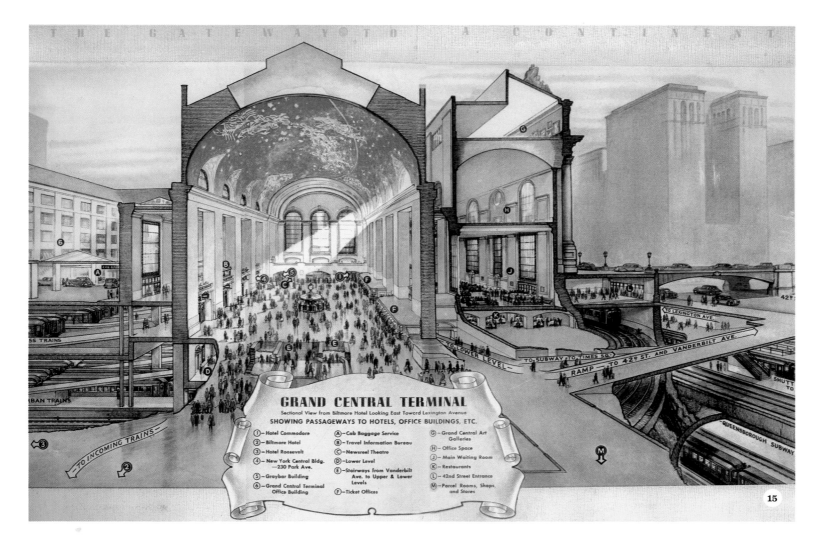

Levels Below Levels

"It is important that the traveler should master the details of the train levels. Briefly they are this: instead of all the trains coming in and going out on the same floor, two levels will be used. The main or express level is for through trains exclusively and is situated on the first floor, under the street. The second level is for suburban traffic only and will be under the express level, the former containing seventeen tracks and the latter forty-two tracks, both connecting with loops which circle under the main terminal building."

—*TOWN & COUNTRY*, JULY 8, 1911

"Express and suburban passengers ... will [be kept separate]. There will consequently be ... much less danger of a flustrated [*sic*] suburbanite running blindly through a seemingly familiar gate to find himself on an express, when it is too late to get off."

—*NEW YORK TIMES*, MARCH 15, 1910

12 Section showing upper and lower levels of tracks beneath Park Avenue.

13, 14 Plans showing the upper and lower levels, including the new loops, February 1912.

15 The complex layers of Grand Central Terminal. *Reprinted from* The Gateway to a Continent, *a New York Central brochure, c. 1939*

Choosing the Architects

In 1903, with Wilgus's conception accepted, the New York Central announced an architectural competition, inviting four firms to submit proposals. Least well-known of the four was Samuel Huckel Jr. of Philadelphia. Best-known were Daniel Burnham of Chicago, and Stanford White, of McKim, Mead & White of New York—nationally prominent architects with major monuments to their credit. The commission went to Reed & Stem of St. Paul, Minnesota, a less well-known firm that specialized in railroad work. The firm often credited with the final design—Warren & Wetmore of New York—never entered the competition at all.

All four competitors had railroad experience of some kind. Two years earlier, Huckel had worked with Wilgus on the new unified waiting room for Grand Central Station. Both Burnham and McKim, Mead & White had just taken on projects for enormous new terminals for the New York Central's great rival, the Pennsylvania Railroad—Burnham's Union Station in Washington, D.C., and McKim, Mead & White's Penn Station on the west side of Manhattan. (McKim and Burnham had only just met for lunch in New York in March of 1903 to compare notes on their respective Penn projects.) Reed & Stem had a lower national profile, but also a great number of railroad stations to their credit—as well as a personal connection to Wilgus, who was Reed's brother-in-law.

No record of Burnham's proposal appears to survive. Huckel doesn't seem to have been a major competitor. McKim, Mead & White and Reed & Stem each proposed grand projects reflecting the current American fashion of classically inspired architecture as idealized in the City Beautiful movement, which dreamed of European-style palaces laid out sym-metrically along grand boulevards. All three surviving proposals included income-producing office buildings above the terminal, but Stanford White sketched out a sixty-story tower that would have captured the title of World's Tallest Building.

Perhaps more than the others, Reed & Stem understood Wilgus's vision of "air rights," as well as the importance of pedestrian circulation both inside and out. The firm's proposal included a grand terminal with an eighteen-story office building rising above it, the whole raised above the city streets on a broad roadway wrapping around the complex, reinstating Park Avenue's north–south trajectory. Inside, in a novel design, the terminal's two levels connected with each other and the streets by a series of sloping ramps. Stretching north from the Terminal, above the now-sunken rail yard, the architects envisioned an extraordinary "Court of Honor"—a fantasy of columned palaces flanking a broad central plaza and ceremonial roadway approaching the terminal—reminiscent of the Court of Honor at the World's Columbian Exposition in Chicago that had given birth to the City Beautiful movement ten years earlier.

New York Central awarded the commission to Reed & Stem. However, Board Chairman William K. Vanderbilt—perhaps with an eye on his Penn Station competition—apparently thought that the architects might not be up to the task of designing such a grand monument, and insisted on bringing in, as collaborators, the firm of Warren & Wetmore, whose principal designer, Whitney Warren, happened to be Vanderbilt's friend, as well as a distant cousin. Warren & Wetmore proposed a low, broad building—with no wraparound roadway or internal ramps—inspired by the Paris that Warren knew from his student days at the École des Beaux-Arts. The design focused on three enormous Roman-style "triumphal arches," meant to suggest the grand entrance to a major city.

The two firms joined forces as the "Associated Architects," but had a difficult relationship, and tussled over the design, which went through various iterations before reaching a final version. The relationship between the firms, bitter from the beginning, ended in a nasty lawsuit. But the resulting Terminal combined the best elements of both concepts, joining Reed & Stem's circulatory plans with Warren & Wetmore's Beaux-Arts–inspired design.

16 Samuel Huckel Jr.'s competition entry.

17 McKim, Mead & White's competition entry. Its sixty-story tower would have made it the world's tallest building. That title was earned instead, and in quick succession, by three downtown New York towers—the Singer (1908), Metropolitan Life (1910), and Woolworth (1913) buildings—all built during the development of Grand Central Terminal. *Courtesy of the New-York Historical Society Collection*

16

17

18 McKim, Mead & White's entry imagined a broad avenue stetching north of the terminal, above an open rail yard, with connecting bridges to rows of palaces on either side. *Courtesy of the New-York Historical Society Collection*

19 Daniel Burnham's Union Station, Washington, D.C., which opened in 1907, might hint at his lost proposal for Grand Central. Like Warren & Wetmore's facade, the design is low and broad, centering on three enormous Roman triumphal arches, c. 1910. *Courtesy of the Library of Congress, Prints and Photographs Division*

20 The tower in McKim, Mead & White's competition entry suggested an updated and enlarged version of White's Madison Square Garden of 1890, which by coincidence had been built on the site of an earlier New York Central depot. *Courtesy of Picture Collection, The New York Public Library, Astor, Lenox and Tilden Foundations*

21 Elements of the unsuccessful design later found their way into the firm's Municipal Building on Chambers Street, completed in 1914.

Designing Architects: Reed & Stem, Warren & Wetmore

"Reed & Stem of St. Paul ... were selected because of their novel suggestion of the substitution of an elevated exterior circumferential driveway with a bridge across 42nd Street, for the interior extension of Park Avenue as shown on the inceptional plan."

—WILLIAM WILGUS, RECORD OF THE INCEPTION AND CREATION OF THE GRAND CENTRAL TERMINAL IMPROVEMENT, 1902–1913

22 Reed & Stem's 1903 design competition submission shows the elevated driveway wrapping around a twenty-story building rising to mansard-roof towers reminiscent of the Commodore's original Depot. *Courtesy of William Wilgus Papers, Manuscripts and Archives Division, New York Public Library, Astor, Lenox and Tilden Foundations*

23 Grand Central's rival: McKim, Mead & White's Pennsylvania Station.

24 Reed & Stem's proposed Court of Honor extended
north from their proposed Terminal along Park
Avenue as far as 50th Street. *Courtesy of William
Wilgus Papers, Manuscripts and Archives Division,
New York Public Library, Astor, Lenox and Tilden
Foundations*

25 The Court of Honor, as built in Chicago at the
World's Columbian Exposition under the supervi-
sion of Daniel Burnham, 1893. *Shepp's World's Fair
Photographed*

"Everyone concedes that the Pennsylvania Railroad has been at extraordinary pains to make its railroad station in this city architecturally beautiful, and that fact may be said to have induced the New York Central Railroad to go to the very large expense of a new terminal building for its own road, conceived also on monumental lines."

—LETTER FROM ENGINEER GUSTAV LINDENTHAL, DECEMBER 21, 1910

26, 27 Whitney Warren (left) and Charles Wetmore, principals of Warren & Wetmore, the firm brought in by William K. Vanderbilt to ensure an appropriately grand design for Reed & Stem's Terminal. *26: Courtesy of the Warren & Wetmore Collection, Avery Architectural & Fine Arts Library, Columbia University; 27: Edward Weeks,* My Green Age, *Little, Brown, 1973*

28 Grand Central Terminal design, 1905. In this early collaboration between Warren & Wetmore and Reed & Stem, the office tower and elevated roadway have disappeared, and Whitney Warren's triumphal arches dominate. *Courtesy of the Picture Collection, New York Public Library, Astor, Lenox and Tilden Foundations*

"In ancient times the entrance to the city was usually decorated and elaborated into an arch of triumph, erected to some naval or military victory or to the glory of some great personage. The city of to-day has no wall surrounding that may serve by elaboration as a pretext to such glorification, but none the less the gateway must exist, and in the case of New York and other cities it is through a tunnel which discharges the human flow into the very centre of the town. Such is the Grand Central Terminal."

—WHITNEY WARREN, QUOTED IN *THE SUN*, FEBRUARY 2, 1913

29 Rome: Arch of Titus. *Photograph by Jean-Christophe Benoist*

30 Rome: Porta San Giovanni. *Photograph by LPLT*

31 New York: Grand Central Terminal. *Photograph by Frank English*

"First Stairless Railway Terminal in History"

— NEW YORK TIMES, FEBRUARY 2, 1913

"There is a whole story in the ramps, how the terminal engineers, not satisfied with theoretical calculations, built experimental ramps at various slopes and studied thereon the gait and gasping limit of lean men with heavy suitcases, fat men without other burden than their flesh, women with babies, school children with books, and all other types of travellers. Upon the data thus obtained they were enabled to construct ramps truly scientific and seductively sloped. Their work, it is said, has given rise to a popular expression on Broadway, 'Well, I'll be ramping.'"

—*NEW-YORK TRIBUNE*, DECEMBER 15, 1912

"Thus has the improvement been completed to accord with the fundamental features proposed in the original inception of 1902, and with an exterior treatment of the station building that displays the architectural ideas of Warren & Wetmore combined with the novel elevated driveway features of Reed & Stem's plan."

—WILLIAM J. WILGUS, RECORD OF THE INCEPTION AND CREATION OF THE GRAND CENTRAL TERMINAL IMPROVEMENT, 1902–1913

32 Rendering showing the ramp leading from the Main Concourse to the Lower Concourse, crossed by a ramp leading from the main concourse to the 42nd Street entrance. Bankers' Magazine, *January 1913*

33 Ramp from the Main Concourse to the Suburban Concourse.

34 Grand Central Terminal as built, 1933.

Demolition

Plans for the demolition of Grand Central Station, including the 1885 Annex, began in 1903, even before the Terminal's architects had been selected. The new Terminal would be a project on a massive scale, involving demolition not just of the station but also of the existing rail yard and the surrounding buildings; excavation not just for building foundations but also for an entire underground maze of double rail yards; and construction not just of the terminal but of the new streets bridging over those yards. Perhaps most remarkable of all: At no point during the entire proj-

ect did train service stop. The Grand Central Palace building on Lexington Avenue was converted into a temporary station—adding a fourth Grand Central to the Terminal's predecessors.

"Perhaps the greatest performance was taking down the old train shed while the rushing traffic went on underneath. The building was of brick, glass, steel and iron, 600 feet long, and having a span of 200 feet. An enormous moving traveler was built to conform to the contour of the train

shed and move on wheels. This traveler was floored over, and had wind shields at one end. The shed was removed in sections of 20 and 40 feet. Work of removal went on during the day, while at night, when regular traffic slackened, work trains came in and carried away the debris. In this manner were removed 1,350 tons of wrought iron, 350 tons of cast iron, 90,000 square feet of corrugated iron, and 60,000 square feet of glass."

—*THE INDEPENDENT,* MARCH 14, 1912

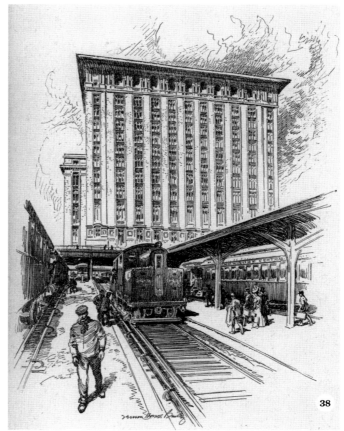

Temporary Terminal

35 Demolition of the Grand Central Station train shed, May 5, 1908.

36 Grand Central Station Annex during demolition, August 15, 1908. Surviving from 1885—because rebuilding the Depot as the Station left it intact—the Annex served as a staging ground for the construction crew and Grand Central staff. In this view can be seen, on the left, the mansard roof of the Annex, designed to match the roof of the old Depot, and, on the right, the redesigned domed towers of the Station that replaced the Depot's mansards.

37 Looking west along 42nd Street from Fourth Avenue, from the fire escape of the Grand Union Hotel, 1910.
· Grand Central Station is down. The Third Avenue Elevated spur is visible at lower right. The Times Tower at Times Square is visible in the distance.

"Anyone who has had occasion to use the Grand Central Station during its process of reconstruction from the show railroad terminal of 1869 into one of the greatest architectural achievements of 1911 could not but marvel that the brain of man could contrive, and still more execute, anything as complicated and practicable as this temporary terminal appears to the initiated. To the layman, the feat of building a great railroad station over and around the old one inconveniencing the traveler to an infinitesimal degree, considering the vastness of the undertaking, appears a project that requires more of God than of man to accomplish. It does not seem as though the completed structure itself can be half as impressive as this remarkable engineering feat of removing old improvements and installing an entire new terminal system without ever altering a train schedule."
—*TOWN & COUNTRY*, JULY 8, 1911

38 To keep train service uninterrupted during the demolition, excavation, and construction of the Terminal, the New York Central set up a temporary terminal in the Grand Central Palace, an exhibition hall on Lexington Avenue at 43rd Street. *Illustration by Vernon Howe Bailey*

Excavation

"One of the features that render the construction of the new Grand Central terminal station a work of unprecedented and monumental proportions, is the vast amount of preliminary excavation that has to be carried out before a single track of the station yard, or a single brick or stone of the station building can be laid. This excavation amounts to a total of over 2,000,000 cubic yards, a large part of which is rock. The blasting out and digging of this material in the heart of a great city, and its removal and disposal many miles from the point of excavation, is in itself a task of huge proportions."

—*SCIENTIFIC AMERICAN*, SEPTEMBER 16, 1905

"Three million cubic yards of excavating have been or are being done, and two-thirds of this has been through solid rock, necessitating blasting, so that the engineers have had constantly to provide against the danger of destroying tracks, crowded trains and buildings. They have had to solve a succession of appalling problems, and their triumph comes near to marking the limit of human achievement."

—*THE INDEPENDENT*, MARCH 14, 1912

39 Excavation of the yard, looking south from 49th Street, 1912.

40 Looking south along Park Avenue towards the Terminal, June 8, 1912.

Building Park Avenue

"The coming of the electric locomotive has ... made a splendid solution of a single growth problem in the largest city of our continent.... a great obstacle to the constant uptown growth of New York has been removed. Sixteen precious city blocks have been given back to the city for development."

—*OUTLOOK*, DECEMBER 28, 1912

"While house wreckers are tearing down the old Grand Central Station the New York Central's staff of engineers and draughtsmen are finishing the plans which will extend Park Avenue northward from the new station to Fifty-seventh Street over what is now a deep gully threaded with the tracks of the new terminal system."

—*NEW YORK TIMES*, JUNE 26, 1910

41 The new Park Avenue and its cross streets—effectively an enormous bridge spread across the sunken train yard—as imagined by Vernon Howe Bailey in *Harper's Weekly*, January 12, 1907.

42 The artist's vision becomes actual steel and concrete. February 2, 1914. Looking north along Park Avenue from East 45th Street.

The Terminal Rises

"Out of what has until lately appeared to the casual traveler to be a confused hole in the ground, criss-crossed by tracks and intermittently shaken by blasts of dynamite, the world's greatest railway terminal is rising in the very heart of New York City."
—*MUNSEY'S MAGAZINE*, APRIL 1911

"The new Grand Central Terminal was thrown wide to the public at midnight last night.... beginning with today, the newest gateway to New York will be ready for the traveling public. Through that gateway in the coming twelvemonth close to 24,000,000 persons will pass on their way to and from the biggest city in the Western World."
—*NEW YORK TIMES*, FEBRUARY 2, 1913

43 January 24, 1912. Looking west along the southern flank of the Terminal.

44 January 24, 1912.

45 March 26, 1912.
Courtesy of the Warren & Wetmore Collection, Avery Architectural & Fine Arts Library, Columbia University

46 May 10, 1912.

3
BEAUX-ARTS SPLENDOR

When the crowds entered Grand Central on February 2, 1913—after ten long years of planning, demolition, and new construction—they found themselves in a miraculous place. Beyond brilliant engineering and planning, the new Terminal offered New Yorkers a sophisticated and beautiful design, combining architecture, sculpture, and painting—all reflecting the latest fashions from Paris.

John B. Snook had modeled the Commodore's Depot after the Louvre. Bradford Gilbert had given the Station more of a French neoclassical look. But the new Terminal took French influence to an entirely new level: a thoroughly Parisian building on a New York avenue, designed by a Paris-trained New York architect who preferred to live in France.

Though just one of many Americans who studied at the École des Beaux-Arts in the French capital, Whitney Warren spent a great deal of time there, imbibing the Gallic approach to architecture. He lived in Paris as a student for a full decade, from 1884 to 1894, and then returned in 1914 and stayed through the end of World War I, during which time he organized the Committee of American Students to support the families of École students sent to the front. He continued to spend time in Paris, on and off, for the rest of his life.

Not only did Warren bring a Parisian sensibility to his own design for the Terminal, based on his years of study at the École, he also arranged for three École-trained Parisians to bring their talents to the project: Jules-Félix Coutan, who designed the monumental sculpture on the 42nd Street facade; Sylvain Salières, who sculpted architectural ornament throughout the complex; and Paul-César Helleu, who sketched out the enormous painting on the ceiling above the Main Concourse. Warren and his colleagues draped modern French style over the latest in American planning and engineering.

"The magnitude of the undertaking, especially the cost... and the wonders of architecture and of luxurious embellishment will of themselves identify this building and its approaches as one of the phenomenal modern structures of the world."
— *WASHINGTON POST,* JANUARY 25, 1913

1 Grand Central Terminal lower level. *Photograph by Patrick Cashin, 2011*

O TRACKS 109

The École des Beaux-Arts

In the United States, the term *Beaux Arts* now refers to an architectural style of the late nineteenth and early twentieth centuries. But to the American architects who studied in Paris at the time, Beaux Arts was the name not of a style but of a school—the École des Beaux-Arts, or School of Fine Arts—and of the method of study it employed.

The École trained France's future artists and architects, but also permitted entry to foreigners who could meet the school's requirements. In Paris, the students' course of study revolved around two poles: the École itself, and an atelier, or workshop. At the École, students attended lectures in such subjects as the history and theory of architecture, ventilation, acoustics, legislation, and contracts. In the atelier, they learned the art of architectural design by sitting at the feet of a master. Students advanced by way of competitions, in which they sketched out designs, often modeled on ancient monuments, that they then developed into detailed projects, in beautifully designed drawings and watercolors. The most advanced students (French only—foreigners weren't eligible) competed each year for the profession's most prestigious student award, the Prix de Rome—the Rome Prize—whose winner spent five years, at government expense, at the French Academy in Rome.

In Warren's day, American students favored certain ateliers, and Warren chose the one led by Honoré Daumet and Charles Louis Girault. Daumet and Girault designed grand public buildings modeled on classical or Renaissance sources, with the oversize columns and arches and elaborate sculptural detail that came to characterize the American Beaux-Arts style. They also paid careful attention to a principle central to all Beaux-Arts architecture: the discipline of planning—both of the careful interior layout of the building and its equally careful arrangement in the urban landscape, preferably placed strategically to create a grand vista.

Back home, Warren became a champion of the Beaux-Arts educational method. In 1894, on his return to New York, he joined several other École alumni in founding the Society of Beaux-Arts Architects—not just, as he was later quoted, "to keep the old crowd together with all its joyous memories," but also "to continue our teachings and traditions, to keep the flame alive and to hand on the torch to those who were to come after us in our own country." He later served as the director of the Beaux-Arts Institute of Design, but was perhaps better known as the organizer of the Beaux Arts Ball, a lavish annual fund-raiser for the Society's educational programs. Warren became one of the great American exponents of the Beaux-Arts style, as well as its methods, and in Grand Central Terminal he created one of New York's finest Beaux-Arts monuments.

"Too many people are accustomed to thinking of the Beaux-Arts student only in the terms which he himself so delights to emphasize—the terms of the Quatz Arts Ball and burning floats and flowing bowls and slim grisettes dancing in renaissance fountains. They forget how prodigiously one must work to have any real spirit for such fantastically abandoned play; and they are generally unaware that the great majority of these same riotous students are paying their own way through the school and working, scores of them, outside while still keeping up with their studies."

—*THE BOOKMAN: A REVIEW OF BOOKS AND LIFE*, OCTOBER 1916 (P. 113)

"The education in architecture in France is above all things artistic.... The object of the French training is to render the student receptive; to make him fruitful in design, and imaginative. By making the training very general in character, it hopes to foster that gift with which all artists should be born, namely, the gift of having ideas."

—*THE BRITISH ARCHITECT*, MARCH 8, 1907 (P .165)

2   École Nationale des Beaux-Arts, rue Bonaparte, Paris, c. 1890. *Photograph by Adolphe Giraudon-Bridgeman Art Library*

Whitney Warren at the École des Beaux-Arts

"In France, a young man who desires to become an architect … joins an atelier…a studio for the study of architecture only, presided over by the master or patron, who is an architect in practice…. In his early days in the atelier he doubtless learns more by the criticism and help freely given him, if he is a good fellow, by the elder pupils, than by the supervision of the master…. But the eye of the master is on him from the first, and as he makes his way forward in the work of the atelier, he finds the relation between master and pupil becomes close, almost paternal…. Once placed, the master becomes to the pupil the chief link which binds him to the great tradition in architecture which the French claim has never been broken with them, and which has descended from master to pupil from the days of the Renaissance…."
—*THE BRITISH ARCHITECT*, MARCH 8, 1907 (P. 165)

3 A drawing of the Church of the Colégio, Ponta Delgada, Azores, by Whitney Warren, 1895, from his student days at the École des Beaux-Arts. *Courtesy of the Cooper-Hewitt, National Design Museum, Smithsonian Institution-Art Resource, NY*

4 The Petit Palais in Paris, designed in 1899 by Charles Louis Girault. *Photograph © Wayne Andrews-Esto*

5 In 1899, Whitney Warren brought the flavor of Daumet and Girault's Paris atelier to Manhattan with one of his first major commissions, the New York Yacht Club, which still stands on West 44th Street. *Photograph by Edwin Levick. Courtesy of The Mariners' Museum. © The facade of the 44th Street NYC clubhouse is a Registered Trademark of the New York Yacht Club*

6

Grand Central Terminal: The Exterior

"Mr. Warren leads the way—literally as well as figuratively, for he is a leggy enthusiast—from his Madison avenue office ... to a point on the southern sidewalk, where the vastness of the terminal building, seen on two sides, properly smites you. There is the facade in gray limestone, with its pillars and triumphal arch windows in triple rows, a group of sculptured figures at the highest centre, and at the extreme corners the stone carved coats-of-arms of New York City and State. There is detailed ornamentation in wreath, oak leaf and other patterns, but all sparingly applied. The style is a modified French Renaissance; the effect is monumental."

—*NEW-YORK TRIBUNE*, DECEMBER 15, 1912 (P. B8)

"Warren & Wetmore present a perspective of the new Grand Central Station for New York ... as visible from Park Avenue. A splendid opportunity is here presented as, placed upon the axis of this important avenue, the entrance may be seen from a distance, a favoring condition seldom found in this congested city."
—*THE ARCHITECT AND BUILDING NEWS*, FEBRUARY 18, 1905

6 Grand Central Terminal facades on Vanderbilt Avenue and East 42nd Street. *Courtesy of the Library of Congress, Prints and Photographs Division*

7 Looking north on Park Avenue from East 38th Street toward Grand Central. The Terminal's unusual siting in the middle of Park Avenue—a serendipitous product of railroad history rather than of architectural design—gave Warren the opportunity to plan the building as the focal point of a typically Beaux-Arts vista set at the end of a broad thoroughfare. *Photograph © Underwood & Underwood/Corbis*

8 Whitney Warren's facade for Grand Central, East 42nd Street facing Park Avenue, photographed in the 1930s. The classical inspiration, the gigantic columns, the overscale arched windows—60 feet tall by 30 feet wide—and the program of monumental sculptural ornament, all mark the Terminal as a product of the Beaux-Arts vision.

9

9, 10 Cornice details, 1988. The attention to ornamental detail, even at the roofline, where it would be barely visible from the street, shows the care lavished on the building's facade, typical of the Beaux-Arts approach. *Photographs by Frank English*

11 The "cornucopia," or "horn of plenty"—symbol of material abundance—in the sculpted ornament at the roof line of the 42nd Street facade. *Photograph by Patrick Cashin*

Heroic Statuary from Paris

"What 'monumental sculpture' really means is shown by the facade recently completed at the Grand Central Terminal in New York City. It is the work of M. Jules Coutan and there is no other group of sculpture so large on the continent."

—CURRENT OPINION, AUGUST 1914

When it came time to commission the grand sculptural group capping the Terminal's 42nd Street facade, Warren passed over American artists, choosing instead the prominent French sculptor Jules-Félix Coutan. President of the Académie des Beaux-Arts and a Prix de Rome winner, Coutan had taught at the École. For the Terminal, he designed an allegorical group of three figures from Roman mythology: Mercury in the center, Hercules on the left, and Minerva on the right. Coutan never left Paris—he created a small-scale model in his studio and sent it to New York, where local craftsmen created the full-scale version to mount atop the Terminal. Once it had been completed and mounted, the fourteen-foot-tall Tiffany clock was installed in its center.

12 The allegorical sculpture atop the 42nd Street facade, designed by Jules-Félix Coutan. *Photograph by Frank English*

"Jules Coutan, the French sculptor ... was chosen by Whitney Warren, the architect, for the execution of a work of art that will be one of the most conspicuous in New York. That American sculptors ... were passed over has been the cause of some criticism, but I do not think American artists are themselves envious on this account."

—*NEW YORK TIMES*, MARCH 31, 1912

13 Jules-Félix Coutan. *Courtesy of Bibliotheque nationale de France*

14 *The Eagle Hunters*, by Jules-Félix Coutan, for the facade of the Muséum national d'histoire naturelle, Paris.

15 Mausoleum for diplomat and journalist José Clemente Paz, La Recoleta Cemetery, Buenos Aires, by Jules-Félix Coutan. *Photograph © Draken. All rights reserved*

16 Coutan's sculptural group at Grand Central, 1957. *Courtesy of the Museum of the City of New York, Arthur Rothstein Collection*

17 Coutan's 1887 statue *La paix armée*, Paris. *Photograph by Nella Buscot*

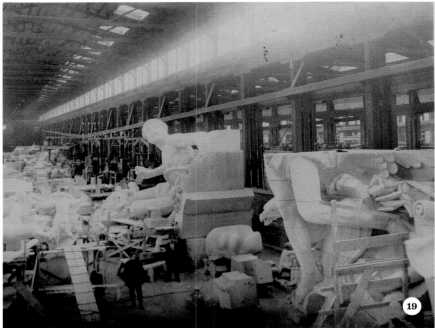

"The physical labor of carving the piece required five months. Begun about December 1 last, it was completed only on May 1. It was done in Long Island City at the stone plant of William Bradley & Son, and, according to Whitney Warren ... it could hardly have been executed anywhere else in the country in a period much short of two years. Its massiveness is the reason. It weighs 1,500 tons, is 66 feet long and 48 feet high. Its central figure, Mercury, is 27 feet 6 inches high and possesses a good right arm weighing tons that extends eleven feet from the body. The big toe and the thumb are each as long as one's forearm.... There is no sculpture like it in this country."

—NEW-YORK TRIBUNE, MAY 31, 1914

"'My general conception,' said the artist, 'is known. The difficulty of the problem which I have before me is to give the vitality of the present to a symbolism that is consecrated by centuries of literature and art and philosophy. I think I shall succeed, but I do not underrate my task....'"

—NEW YORK TIMES, MARCH 31, 1912

18 Model by Jules-Félix Coutan, c. 1912, which sat in Whitney Warren's office. *Courtesy of the Warren & Wetmore Collection, Avery Architectural & Fine Arts Library, Columbia University*

19 Carving the statuary from Indiana Sandstone in Long Island City, c. 1913. *Courtesy of the Queens Borough Public Library, Long Island Division, August Kruzensk Photographs*

20 The individual elements of the group, separately carved, could be united only when mounted on the Terminal. *Courtesy of the Queens Borough Public Library, Long Island Division, August Kruzenk Photographs*

"Mr. Warren has written a brief interpretation of the group's significance: '... a monument to the glory of commerce as typified by Mercury, supported by moral and mental energy—Hercules and Minerva. All to attest that this great enterprise has grown and exists, not merely from the wealth expended, nor by the revenue derived, but by the brain and brawn constantly concentrated upon its development for nearly a century.'"
—*NEW YORK TIMES*, FEBRUARY 2, 1913

" The carving was done in a great inclosed shed running down to the edge of the channel of the East River on the east side of Blackwell's Island. Electric cranes travel through its length with twenty-five ton stones as if they were children's blocks…. When they were all set down the pile was more than sixty-six feet long and upward of fifty feet high. Then the pneumatic carving tools were brought out and, guided by the hands of a dozen or more highly skilled artisans, the secret hidden behind the elemental and jagged front of the mass gradually came to light."
—*NEW-YORK TRIBUNE*, MAY 31, 1914

21 At work on Hercules, c. 1914. © *Photograph Paul Thompson/National Geographic Society/Corbis*

"[New York Central] President Newman was in Paris and went to see Jules Coutan.... Although this was several years ago, the design closely resembled the group now executed. 'How soon do you think you will have it finished?' asked the railroad official, as he glanced over the drawing. 'About two years.' 'Good heavens!' exclaimed Mr. Newman, 'we've got to have this in four months.' 'I am not a speculator,' responded the sculptor. 'All the pleasure I shall ever get out of this will be in doing it right.' Evidently the sculptor had his way."

—*NEW-YORK TRIBUNE*, MAY 31, 1914

"[Coutan, asked if he would now visit the United States:] 'I have no such desire. From what I have learned pictorially of the characteristics of your country, especially with reference to the standards of art, I do not think that it would interest me. In fact, I should wish rather to avoid it. I fear that the sight of some of your architecture would distress me.'"

—*NEW YORK TIMES*, MARCH 31, 1912

22, 23 Detail of Minerva, left, and Hercules, right, 2005. *Photographs by Frank English*

24 Installation of the Coutan statuary, July 11, 1914, more than a year after completion of the Terminal. *Courtesy of the Warren & Wetmore Collection, Avery Architectural & Fine Arts Library, Columbia University*

25 The 14-foot-tall Tiffany clock—the world's largest bearing that name—sits at the center of Coutan's sculpted group. Tiffany, famed for its inimitable colored glass, also manufactured some of the world's most exclusive timepieces. The clock face, framed in brass, incorporates a sunburst design in the central round glass panel. Roman numerals are set in convex red glass circles. *Photograph by Frank English, 2006*

Pershing Square Viaduct

Whitney Warren didn't design the Terminal with a single French building in mind. He did, however, model the Pershing Square Viaduct—which lifts Park Avenue up and over 42nd Street, to connect with the outer drive around the Terminal—after Paris's Alexander III bridge. Completed in 1900, for the same Exposition at which the Gare d'Orsay introduced underground electric railroading, the Paris bridge included a sculptural group, *France in the Renaissance,* designed by Coutan. In Paris, Coutan's sculpture adorns the Alexander bridge; in New York, Coutan's sculpture looks out over Warren's version of that same bridge.

"Traffic will be carried over Forty-second Street at this level by a bridge, which will be an exact copy of the famous Alexander III Bridge over the River Seine in Paris. This structure, which was erected several years ago in honor of Alexander III of Russia, is said to be one of the most beautiful in the world."
—*NEW YORK TIMES*, MARCH 4, 1910

26 Alexander III bridge, Paris with sculpture by Jules-Félix Coutan.

27 Pershing Square Viaduct over 42nd Street, New York. Though always part of the plan for carrying Park Avenue traffic around the Terminal, and designed by Warren & Wetmore in 1912, the 600-foot-long viaduct was not completed until 1919. As originally conceived, the viaduct had tall pylons similar to those on its Parisian model. All three of its arches were originally open; today the central arch encloses a restaurant.
Photograph by Patrick Cashin, 2012

Grand Central Interiors

TO ALL THOSE WHO WITH HEAD HEART AND HAND
TOILED IN THE CONSTRUCTION OF THIS MONUMENT TO
THE PUBLIC SERVICE. THIS IS INSCRIBED

28

Grand Central's interior spaces overwhelm the visitor with their vast spaciousness, handsome materials, and exquisite attention to detail. The main areas are simply arranged: a huge waiting room just off 42nd Street—from which a ramp slopes down to the cathedral-like Main Concourse, with raised balconies at the east and west ends—and the Suburban Concourse directly below. All other rooms are secondary. The architects chose three materials with which to line these spaces: imitation Caen stone for the walls, Botticino marble for decorative wall trim, and Tennessee marble for the floors. Because actual Caen stone was too expensive, the architects used an approximation made of Portland cement, lime, sand, and plaster. Warren & Wetmore considered the result fine enough to use in the 52nd Street mansion they designed for William K. Vanderbilt.

The huge spaces of the Main Concourse and waiting room are lit by daylight from enormous window openings and by electric light from huge bronze chandeliers ("electroliers") hanging from the ceiling. The Concourse is open and unobstructed, with the exception of a centrally placed, circular information kiosk topped by a spherical, four-faced brass clock—used for a century by countless New Yorkers as an easily found meeting place amid the endless motion in the Terminal.

"All through the main rooms and corridors a soft toned Italian marble has been lavishly used and the exquisiteness of the detail may be gathered from the fact that the famous Rookwood pottery of Cincinnati has furnished certain of the ornamental motifs over the doors. Other doorways are surmounted by great bronze clocks set in a frame work of sculptured marble and in the corridors are the enormous bronze electroliers, suspended by bronze chains.... The main concourse is a magnificent room, finished in Botticino marble and buff-tinted stone and with a great domed ceiling.... Nothing finer has been done in New York."

—*TOWN & COUNTRY*, JANUARY 25, 1913

29

30

28 Entrance vestibule at 42nd Street, with inscription, c. 1990s. *Photograph by Frank English*

29 Main Waiting Room, c. 1913 (renamed Vanderbilt Hall in 1998). *Courtesy of the Library of Congress, Prints and Photographs Division, Detroit Publishing Company Collection*

30 Main Concourse, December 16, 1914.

"No individual could have been or was responsible for this work as a whole. It is the organic combination of the brain and brawn of many men. Those chiefly concerned would be the last to accept any award of sole personal credit. The inscription over the Forty-second Street entrance to the main waiting room, suggested by Miles Bronson, now terminal manager, and approved by W. H. Newman, then President, has long been accepted by those associated in the enterprise as most appropriate and adequate."
—*NEW YORK TIMES*, LETTER TO THE EDITOR
FROM ALFRED FELLHEIMER, NOVEMBER 22, 1926

"The main waiting-room will be two hundred feet long, eighty feet wide, and fifty feet high. The walls will be cream-colored; and, save for maps of the two railroad systems using the terminal, will be bare of adornment. The idea behind this simplicity is best expressed by one of the architects who said to me: 'It is not to be an art museum, or a hall of fame, but a place of dignified simplicity, easy of access and comfortable.'"
—*MUNSEY'S MAGAZINE*, APRIL 1911

"Here is a space like the nave of an Old World cathedral. It compels to silence. A solitary visitor would feel himself belittled; a few persons could not make themselves at home in this tremendous amplitude, which is almost an architectural satire on man. A multitude will doubtless be able to use it without having sentimental qualms."
—*NEW-YORK TRIBUNE*, DECEMBER 15, 1912

31 Main Concourse west balcony and grand staircase, 1913. *Courtesy of the Library of Congress, Prints and Photographs Division, Detroit Publishing Company Collection*

32 Lobby and grand staircase of the Paris Opera. Grand Central mirrors the plan and organization of the Paris space, but shows relative restraint in the application of decorative ornament.

"'I was surprised when I went into the Grand Central Terminal the other day, when looking up I saw only stone vaulted ceilings ... but with simple lines, giving the effect of a great thing easily achieved. Here it seemed one saw a great edifice resting on nothing, as it were.... It is a tremendous thing for your art when you accomplish great effects with nothing but simple lines.... If you aim for good lines only, and get them, as has been done in the Terminal, then you may add all the decoration you wish without spoiling your building.'"

—*NEW YORK TIMES*, QUOTING VISITING FRENCH ARCHITECT ACHILLE DUCHÈNE, DECEMBER 26, 1912

"'A station,' said Mr. Warren, 'should be fool-proof; there should be no possible way of making a mistake.... Once having entered the station the traveler should find himself in a large vestibule and, theoretically, directly in front of the Information Bureau, so that in case he does not know his way about and cannot read the various signs he may address himself and be properly directed without loss of time and encumbering space.'"
—*NEW YORK TIMES*, FEBRUARY 9, 1913

"The outbound concourse, the principal feature of the main building, is a magnificent room.... Only when standing under its vaulted ceiling can its impressive proportions be appreciated and even then one hardly realizes that it could accommodate fifteen regiments of infantry. It is finished in Botticino marble and buff-tinted stone which, under the light that falls softly through six great dome-shaped windows, gives a most pleasing and cheery effect."
—*BANKERS' MAGAZINE*, JANUARY 1913

"The most beautiful and striking feature of the suburban level is the main ramp from the subway to the concourse. It is a marble corridor forty feet wide descending at a gentle slope between the main waiting-room and concourse. Its location between these two rooms with their lofty ceiling gives it an impressive height. It is flanked by the great columns of the main concourse through which a glimpse of the beautiful room is had. The sunlight falls softly through windows high above and by night the walk is illuminated by five mammoth bronze electroliers of wondrous beauty and ornate design, suspended by ornamental bronze chains."
—*BANKERS' MAGAZINE*, JANUARY 1913

33 Main Concourse, seen from the west balcony, 1913. *Courtesy of the Library of Congress, Prints and Photographs Division, Detroit Publishing Company Collection*

34 Information booth as originally built, without windows or roof. *Courtesy of the Warren & Wetmore Collection, Avery Architectural & Fine Arts Library, Columbia University*

35 Ramp from the Main Concourse to the Suburban Concourse. *Courtesy of the Library of Congress, Prints and Photographs Division, Detroit Publishing Company Collection*

"Underneath the main concourse is the suburban concourse, which is about the same dimensions excepting as to the height of the ceiling. It is laid out in the same convenient manner and provides the same facilities as the main concourse. In planning this great terminal the railroad company has given particular consideration to the comfort and convenience of suburban passengers, affording them the same facilities as the through travellers enjoy."

—*BANKERS' MAGAZINE*, JANUARY 1913

36 Main Concourse ticket windows with their original bronze grilles, and the original hanging light fixtures, as well as bronze luggage rails below, c. 1930s. *Photograph by Edward O. Bagley*

37 Suburban Concourse, c. 1913. *Courtesy of the Library of Congress, Prints and Photographs Division, Detroit Publishing Company Collection*

Guastavino Vaulting and Underground Dining

The herringbone patterns in the vaulting of the Oyster Bar & Restaurant aren't just decorative—they belong to an unusual structural system generally known as Guastavino vaults, or Guastavino tiles, named for Rafael Guastavino, an immigrant architect from Spain who brought the technique with him to New York. Guastavino's patented system of fireproof vaulting using thin tile and cement, based on time-honored Catalan techniques, became remarkably popular in the decades just before and after 1900—it was used everywhere from underground subway stations to the enormous dome of the Cathedral Church of Saint John the Divine. At Grand Central Terminal, Warren & Wetmore used Guastavino tiles at the Oyster Bar to create the look of a Central European *keller*, or cellar: a low, vaulted basement room for serving food and alcohol—Warren would have known such places from his student days. Vaulted basement restaurants had become popular in New York and were often included in new midtown hotels. Contemporaneously with Grand Central, Warren & Wetmore used Guastavino vaulting in another basement restaurant with a Vanderbilt connection: the grillroom and bar, called the Crypt, in the lower floors of the Vanderbilt Hotel at Four Park Avenue, just a few blocks south of the Terminal.

"Adjoining the concourse on the suburban level is the restaurant which has been planned with great care and in which every appointment will be of the best. Ordinarily a station restaurant does not appeal strongly to travellers. This one will be as fine as any in the best hotels in point of service and equipment.... It is such an inviting room, being artistically treated by a series of Gustavino [*sic*] arches of cream colored tile, giving a grotto like effect, that no one will want to pass without taking a meal."
—*BANKERS' MAGAZINE*, JANUARY 1913

38 The Grand Central Terminal Restaurant (Oyster Bar), c. 1913. *Courtesy of the Library of Congress, Prints and Photographs Division, Detroit Publishing Company Collection*

39 Entrance to the Oyster Bar, 2012. The vaulted, tiled Guastavino ceiling unexpectedly carries sound between opposite corners, earning this space the nickname "the Whispering Gallery." *Photograph by Frank English*

The Sky Above: Paul-César Helleu

"It must have taken courage in Mr. Warren, the architect, to call in for the solution of his ceiling problem an artist not hitherto known, publicly at all events, as a decorator. He has had his reward.... M. Helleu has made a remarkably good ceiling ... simply painted a lovely blue, and against this cloudless sky the signs of the Zodiac are delicately indicated in gold.... His light, airy scheme, fragile as it is in its essential quality, nevertheless fits constructively into the vast architectural ensemble. Both for its intrinsic merit, its delicate, distinguished beauty, and for its significance as in some sort a protest against the conventional, overpainted decoration, it is heartily to be welcomed."
—*NEW-YORK TRIBUNE*, FEBRUARY 16, 1913

40

The architects had originally thought to open the ceiling to the heavens with actual skylights, but that proved impractical. Instead, yet another Parisian, Paul-César Helleu, designed a Zodiac to arch across the Concourse ceiling. A friend of painters Claude Monet, James Abbott McNeill Whistler, and John Singer Sargent, as well as writer Marcel Proust (who might have modeled the painter Elstir, in *À la recherche du temps perdu*, on his friend), Helleu had studied at the École a quarter of a century before Warren. Best known for his etched portraits of women, including William K. Vanderbilt's daughter Consuelo, Helleu came to New York in 1913 for a three-month stay to carry out several portrait commissions, but also to find eight beautiful American women whose portraits he would render for a Parisian weekly (as well as for a "Special Pictorial Section" of the *New York Times*). While here, he sketched out a concept of the Concourse ceiling for Warren, but left the execution to a pair of New York scenic designers, J. Monroe Hewlett and Charles Basing.

With a team of fifty assistants, Hewlett and Basing—who had both also studied in Paris—painted the entire expanse, and on Helleu's instructions included some sixty electric bulbs of varying strength to add to the starry effect. The New York Central proudly announced that the resulting ceiling, designed in consultation with a Columbia professor of astronomy, could profitably be studied by schoolchildren—until a starstruck commuter noticed that, with the exception of Orion, the empyrean had been painted backward. Various explanations have been advanced to explain the mistake, but the design remained unchanged, despite an opportunity to correct it that arose in the 1940s, when the deteriorated ceiling had to be replaced. On a set of rock-board sheets anchored into the ceiling, Charles Gulbrandsen—a former associate of Hewlett's—re-created the original design, with the same backward orientation. Said Gulbrandsen, "The ceiling is decoration, not a map. The constellations are north. They should be south. So what?"

40 Paul-César Helleu in his Paris atelier. *Photograph © Les Amis de Paul-César Helleu*

41 Helleu's portrait of Consuelo Vanderbilt, 1900. Helleu painted Ms. Vanderbilt again on his 1912 visit to New York, when he designed the ceiling of the Main Concourse. *Courtesy of the National Portrait Gallery, Smithsonian Institution/Art Resource, NY*

42 The original ceiling, seen from the west balcony, c. 1913.

"... a picture of wondrous beauty ..."

"The entire work of M. Helleu, whether it be in painting, pastel, dry-point or drawing, may be described as a tender and fervent hymn to woman's beauty."
—*PARISIAN ILLUSTRATED REVIEW*, JANUARY 1901

"'Fortunately there are no seats in the concourse,' remarked one of the railway officials on the inspection tour, 'or I would fear that some passengers might miss their trains while contemplating this starry picture.'"
—*NEW YORK TIMES*, JANUARY 29, 1913

"Mr. Warren, who had been hearing a deal of compliment on the superb ceiling of the new terminal's concourse, was willing to say of it simply: 'It fills the bill. After all, that's what a thing must do architecturally.... When we decided upon a flat, hung ceiling it became a question of decoration. All decoration means something if it is appropriate....' 'And the starry ceiling,' his interviewer suggested, 'reflects the guidance of travelers of old?' Mr. Warren assented."
—*NEW YORK TIMES*, FEBRUARY 9, 1913

"A one-time student of Galland, the great French architect, scene painter and painter of allegorical figures, the all-round decorator and rival of Puvis de Chavannes, possibly the best equipped artist of his time for this character of work—Mr. J. Monroe Hewlett, architect of this city."
—*TOWN & COUNTRY*, NOVEMBER 23, 1912

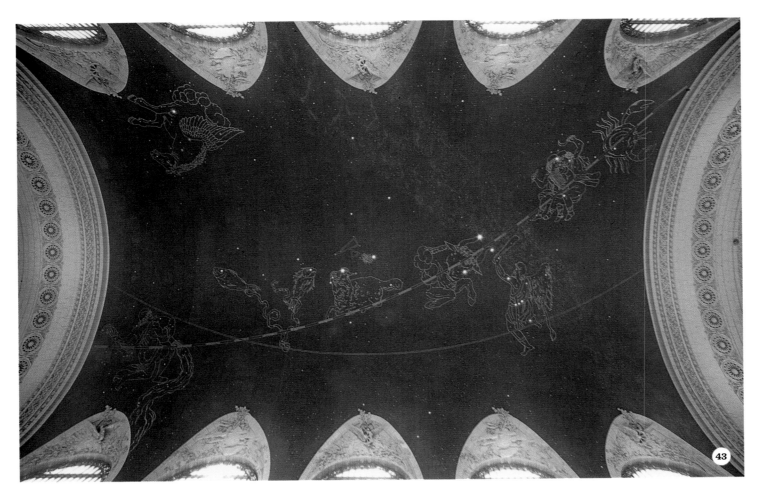

43

44

"The dominant note of the color scheme is a turquoise blue such as one sees in the sky of Greece and of southern Italy. The contour of the ceiling produces a gradation of tone that gives an effect of illimitable space. As one passes down the incline to the suburban concourse and catches a glimpse of the ceiling … there is revealed a picture of wondrous beauty and so startlingly natural that one for the moment imagines himself in some old building of Pompeii having no ceiling save the blue sky itself. The view presented is a section of the heavens as seen during the months from October to March, or from Aquarius to Cancer. Sweeping across the ceiling from east to west are two broad bands of gold, representing the Ecliptic and the Equator."

—*RAILWAY AND LOCOMOTIVE ENGINEERING*, MARCH 1913

"There are 2,500 stars of various magnitudes, while the great stars which mark the signs and constellations, some sixty-three of them, will be illuminated by electricity."

—*NEW YORK TIMES*, JANUARY 29, 1913

43 The ceiling after its restoration, c. 1999. *Photograph by Frank English*

44 Detail, c. 1999, showing Aries (the Ram). The band of gold connecting the signs represents the Ecliptic, the path of the sun. *Photograph by Frank English*

Ornament in Bronze and Stone

45 *Hommage au Maitre Whitney Warren—S. Salières.* The sculptor, posing in front of an earlier version of the horn of plenty sculpture supporting Coutan's mythical group (the inscription, "The Grand Central Terminal," differs slightly from the final version). *Courtesy of the Warren & Wetmore Collection, Avery Architectural & Fine Arts Library, Columbia University*

"**[Salières carvings] are notable on account of their departure from the conventional ornamentation of buildings and their appropriateness to a railway station. They are handled with admirable restraint and sense of composition, although in places they fairly seem to spill from the stone of the building. In an original way they symbolize commerce and its consequent abundance. The pine, the oak, the olive, corn, the grape, the fruits of the American subtropics, are interwound with the serpent, taken from Mercury's wand and emblematic of commerce, together with the winged wheel, representing speed, the signal flags typifying safety, and the trumpet emblematic of progress, all appear in the carvings.**"

—*CHRISTIAN SCIENCE MONITOR*, AUGUST 8, 1914

Warren's third Parisian import, Sylvain Salières, was another Prix de Rome winner. But unlike Jules-Félix Coutan, who would not deign to visit New York, and Helleu, who came for a few months of high-profile commissions but then returned to Paris, Salières worked in New York for five years and then moved to the Carnegie Institute of Technology in 1916, holding the position of head of the School of Sculpture until his death in 1920.

Salières's work at the Terminal ranges from the carved ornament and inscriptions above and below the Tiffany clock on the 42nd Street facade, and the enormous sculpted winged wheels in the lunettes on the north wall of the Main Concourse, to the ornamental bands on the ceiling of the Main Waiting Room, elaborate metalwork on window grilles, window frames, doorways, and moldings throughout the complex.

The details of Salières's ornament vary, but often focus on acorns and oak leaves, because those were the chosen symbols of the Vanderbilt family. Though the name Vanderbilt today suggests vast and ancient wealth, the Commodore came from humble roots, and the family had no coat of arms. Vanderbilt selected the acorn as the family symbol, and adopted the old saying "Great oaks from little acorns grow" as the family motto. William K. Vanderbilt's wife, Alva, later incorporated acorns into the new coat of arms she designed for the family.

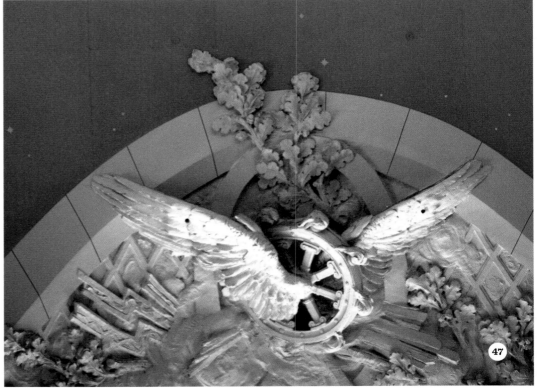

46 Elevator metalwork. Salières's leaf and acorn designs in bronze above and wrought-iron grille below. *Photograph by Frank English, 2010*

47 Ornamental sculpture by Salières above the lunettes in the Main Concourse. The winged wheel, suggesting transportation, intertwines with Vanderbilt oak-tree foliage. *Photograph by Frank English, 1998*

48 Vanderbilt acorns and oak leaves. *Photograph by Frank English*

49 *Photograph by Frank English*

50 Salières's carved wreaths around the fountains under the west stairs in the Main Concourse include loving portraits of Vanderbilt's acorns. *Photograph by Brett Dion, 2012*

Electric Chandeliers

The Sterling Bronze Company created the enormous electric chandeliers hanging from the ceiling in the Main Waiting Room and the Main Concourse. Those in the waiting room, weighing 2,500 pounds apiece, hold 132 bulbs in four tiers, surrounded by oak leaves. The chandeliers in the Main Concourse, weighing 800 pounds, hold more than one hundred bulbs. All can be lowered by motorized winches when necessary for cleaning and bulb replacement. Similar but more modest light fixtures hang from ceilings or are attached to walls throughout the Terminal. A close inspection of their elaborate, Beaux-Arts-inspired floral ornament will generally reveal acorns and oak leaves.

51 Chandelier detail, north balcony. *Photograph by Frank English, 1988*

52 Details of the chandelier on the north balcony, with acorns and oak leaves. *Photograph by Frank English, 2008*

53 A restored chandelier awaits its reinstallation in Vanderbilt Hall, c, 1992. *Photograph by Frank English*

54 Chandelier reflected in the window, Main Concourse. *Photograph by Frank English, 2006*

Information Desk Clock

55 After the Tiffany clock on the 42nd Street facade, the best known of the Terminal's many clocks is the four-faced ball clock on the information booth in the center of the Main Concourse. The Self Winding Clock Company of Brooklyn built the original brass timepiece and then rebuilt its works in the 1950s. Each opaline glass clock face is illuminated from within. Note the large cast Vanderbilt acorn at the very top. *Photograph by Patrick Cashin*

4

A SPECIAL PLACE IN THE CITY

Beyond providing an architecturally splendid entrance to the metropolis, the new Grand Central Terminal developed as a mass transit hub, shaped an entire new section of New York, and in the process made a place for itself unlike any other in the city.

In the Commodore's day, Grand Central lay far out of town—most disembarking passengers boarded horse-drawn carriages for the journey south to the city center. To the north lay the open train yards, taking up a sizable piece of Manhattan. Fourth Avenue existed north of the yards, but construction of the Annex severed the avenue's connection with its continuation south of 42nd Street.

By 1913, Grand Central lay at the heart of midtown Manhattan. Whether below ground with the new IRT subway, above ground with the old Third Avenue Elevated, or at ground level with streetcars, the Terminal functioned as the center of a web of interconnecting mass transit rail routes. At the same time, with the train yard sunk below street level, the new complex stood at the center of a newly developing district, Terminal City, imagined by its promoters as New York's next civic center. And with its unusual location on axis with Park Avenue, with planning underway for the Pershing Square Viaduct that would surround it with elevated roadways, Grand Central carved out its own special place in the anonymous urban grid.

1 *Photograph by Frank English*

Mass Transit Crossroads

The new Grand Central Terminal offered passengers on its express and commuter lines access to New York's mass transit via rails at every level.

The Third Avenue Elevated, connecting the Battery to 120th Street, began service in 1878, and from the start included a two-block-long spur leading west past Lexington Avenue to the recently completed Grand Central Depot. The Elevated survived until 1955, but the spur closed in 1923, ten years after the Terminal's completion.

Below ground, the original IRT subway, which opened in 1904, connected lower Manhattan with Grand Central before turning west to Times Square and then north up Broadway. With the subway and Terminal under development simultaneously, some planners thought it possible to link the two, and suggested the Terminal be designed so arriving commuter trains could actually transfer onto the tracks of the IRT and continue downtown as local mass transit. That proved impractical, so efforts focused instead on making the commuters' connection to the subway as seamless as possible, by creating an interior mezzanine corridor connecting the Terminal's incoming station, now the Biltmore Room, to the IRT.

For surface transportation, electric streetcars— once a big part of the city's mass transit system— passed by the Terminal on tracks embedded in the 42nd Street pavement, while on Park Avenue they descended into a former railway tunnel between 41st and 34th streets. Some streetcars continued through the Steinway (or Belmont) Tunnel beneath the East River, to Queens. Eventually that tunnel served the IRT Flushing Line that later, with a western extension, connected to Times Square, while the tunnel beneath Park Avenue was converted to automobile use.

2

"**Grand Central Terminal is the center of the most extensive combination of passenger transportation lines in the world. On Forty-second street there will be the completion of the Belmont Tunnel to Long Island, the Hudson & Manhattan Tunnels to New Jersey and the Lexington Avenue Subway, four great arteries of local transit, including the present Interborough Subway, having direct sub-surface connections with both the outgoing and incoming stations of Grand Central Terminal. In addition, electric surface lines, radiating in all directions, pass the door.... There is thus established an intercommunication of travel between the New York Central Lines and the lines of local transit that places every nook and corner of Greater New York, Long Island and Jersey City in direct touch with this great railway terminal.**"

—*BANKERS' MAGAZINE*, JANUARY 1913

Above Ground: "Another busy place ..."

"**The demolition of the elevated railroad spur on Forty-second Street ... was celebrated yesterday by a parade and a luncheon at the Hotel Commodore.... Speakers at the luncheon predicted that the work was the initial step in the removal of all elevated railway structures in the city.... Headed by a platoon of mounted policemen and the Municipal Band of sixty pieces, members ... marched south over the viaduct to Fortieth Street.**"

—*NEW YORK TIMES*, MAY 23, 1924

2 The Third Avenue elevated spur seen from Park Avenue, with motorcars approaching Grand Central, prior to construction of the Pershing Square Viaduct, 1915. *Photograph by G. W. Pullis*

Below Ground

"About eighty percent of the people arriving at and departing from the terminal use the subway."
—*BANKER'S MAGAZINE*, JANUARY, 1913

3   The IRT Lexington Avenue line station at Grand Central, a major stop on New York's first subway route, 1952.

4   The Steinway (or Belmont) Tunnel, connecting Grand Central Terminal to Queens, and the route of its eventual extension west to Times Square. *Courtesy of the* New York Times, *September 17, 1916*

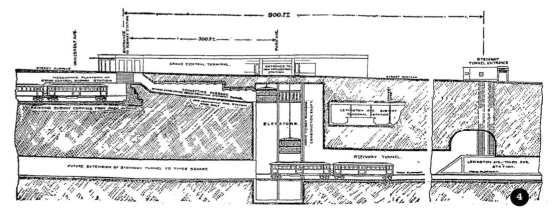

Street Level

"Automobiles will be coursing soon through the section of the Park Avenue tunnel ... recently abandoned by street car traffic.... Park Avenue is an epitome of the history of transportation on the American continent. Stage coaches, omnibuses, horse cars, locomotives, electric trolleys and finally high-powered automobiles have traveled this old Indian trail."

—*NEW YORK TIMES*, SEPTEMBER 15, 1935

A Special Place in the City

"Park Avenue will be extended from its present high level at Fortieth street. It is to bridge Forty-second street and in a broad plaza swing around the great new station structure."

—*FREIGHT: THE SHIPPERS' FORUM*, AUGUST 1910

5 A streetcar on the 42nd Street crosstown line, passing in front of Grand Central Terminal, 1946.

6 Streetcars on Park Avenue, seen from 41st Street, in 1907, with Grand Central Station on the left, the old Depot Annex on the right, and the entrance to the elevated spur between them. The streetcar tracks lead into a tunnel, running beneath Park Avenue, south to 34th Street.

7 Same view, with the Terminal having replaced the Station and Depot Annex, 1915. In 1935, with streetcar service discontinued, the city tore up the tracks and repaved the tunnel for automobile use.

8 Park Avenue looking south from the Terminal; streetcars entering the tunnel, with the Grand Union Hotel on the left and the Belmont Hotel on the right, c. 1913.

9 Same view, 2009. *Photograph by Frank English*

In Manhattan's two-hundred-year-old street grid, the island's avenues extend for miles to the north and south with almost no interruption. The only exception in midtown Manhattan is Park Avenue, originally cut in two by the Grand Central train yards. Whitney Warren took advantage of the situation to design the Terminal as a Beaux-Arts monument on axis with the avenue, but with the development of midtown and the extension of Park Avenue above the yards north of the Terminal, traffic flow demanded that Park Avenue be reconnected.

Two special short north–south arteries flanking the Terminal originally tried to accommodate Park Avenue traffic: Vanderbilt Avenue on the west and Depew Place on the east, each named for a Grand Central creator. Automobile trips along a unified Park Avenue had to wait for completion of the Pershing Square Viaduct across 42nd Street which, though planned with the Terminal's design, remained unbuilt until 1919. Eventually, the viaduct would lift northbound traffic up and over 42nd Street, around the new Terminal, and back down onto Park Avenue, extending above the train yards. The roadways around the Terminal opened to traffic only gradually, first on the west side along Vanderbilt Avenue, and then later, on the east side along Depew Place, as far as 45th Street. The construction of the New York Central Building in 1928, extending the roadways one block farther to 46th Street, completed the full viaduct system. Each step of the process brought parades and celebratory luncheons, as the viaducts finally opened Park Avenue completely from end to end.

Today, Grand Central sits within this remarkable environment—a large urban complex breaking out of the grid, flanked by its own special streets, and surrounded by elevated roadways. Nothing comparable exists anywhere else in Manhattan.

" ... an uninterrupted thoroughfare ... "

"Property owners ... with city officials, will celebrate next Wednesday the opening of Park Avenue as a completed thoroughfare from Astor Place to the Harlem River.... The steel viaduct extending from Fortieth to Forty-second Streets is in some respects the most noteworthy portion of the Park Avenue improvement.... This roadway leads to a high-level roadway on the west side of the Terminal Building that is 35 feet in width and is in reality an upper story of Vanderbilt Avenue. On the east side of the Terminal Building there is also a high-level roadway ... but for the present the public is excluded ... because it is legally a private right of way."

—*NEW YORK TIMES*, APRIL 13, 1919

10 Far above the unique thoroughfare that is the elevated roadway of Park Avenue, 2006. *Photograph by Frank English*

11 Drawing of the proposed viaduct and Commodore Hotel by Vernon Howe Bailey. *Courtesy of the* New York Times, *November 26, 1916*

"The din of motor and streetcar traffic on Forty-second Street, the shunt and shuffle of pedestrians, the upward thrust of the buff and yellow skyscrapers around the terminal, produce an impact not easily forgotten."

—*WPA GUIDE TO NEW YORK CITY*, 1939

"An old lady with a touch of lavender to her costume and a general air of having come down from Boston on the one-o'clock train accosted a traffic cop outside of Grand Central. 'Pardon me,' she said, pitching her voice above the noise of the traffic. 'Can you tell me, please, what has become of Park Avenue?'"

—*NEW YORKER*, FEBRUARY 26, 1944

12 A bird's-eye view of the viaduct over 42nd Street, 2005. *Photograph by Frank English*

13 The elevated roadway along Vanderbilt Avenue, 2010. *Photograph by Frank English*

Civic Center

"The term 'Grand Central' no longer designates a mere railroad station, but a large and impressive civic center.... Where there were formerly smoking tracks and four-story buildings, there are large handsome structures—office buildings, stores, hotels, apartments and clubs. ... In fact, the whole surrounding neighborhood now goes by the name of the Grand Central District, and is one of the chief business centers of the metropolis."
—*ENGINEERING NEWS-RECORD*, SEPTEMBER 9, 1920

"Right in the centre of New York stands a group of connected buildings that are unique in the world's history. A man born in one of these buildings could live, carry on a large business and enjoy life's comforts and luxuries without ever emerging from beneath a roof.... [It] consists of Grand Central Terminal and the buildings which can be reached from this massive central structure without setting foot outdoors. In this unit may be found every kind of food and clothing a human being needs, great banks, restaurants, stores of all descriptions ... and even picture galleries. It contains world-famous chefs, renowned orchestras, roof gardens and one of the largest ballrooms in the world. But all this has grown up so gradually before the eyes of New York's citizens that they have not realized the wonder that is in their midst."
—*NEW YORK TIMES*, AUGUST 29, 1926

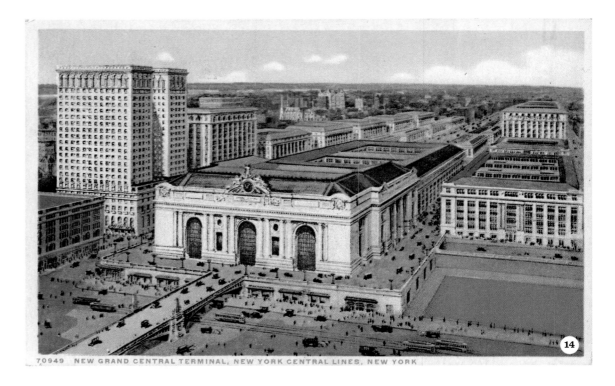

70949 NEW GRAND CENTRAL TERMINAL, NEW YORK CENTRAL LINES, NEW YORK

The new Grand Central Terminal, as conceived by William Wilgus, brought an opportunity—unprecedented in the city's history—to build an entirely new district on dozens of newly created blocks. But the New York Central's architects, engineers, and planners accomplished far more than just a new real estate development. They took an unsightly and dangerous train yard with miles of track, sank it underground, and erected above it a vast steel structure supporting the city's newest business center of hotels, skyscrapers, and exhibition halls, all linked below ground and interconnecting with the Terminal. Then, in place of a motley collection of buildings facing the tracks, they created a beautifully landscaped boulevard lined with the city's most fashionable apartment buildings. And because one firm, Warren & Wetmore, designed so many of the buildings, and supervised the work of other architects working in the new zone, the New York Central could coordinate an overall urban form and uniform architectural style for what the New York Central called Terminal City.

The plan emerged only gradually. Wilgus's conception focused strictly on the financial value of the new development, which he saw as underwriting the cost of the entire building and electrification project. Reed & Stem's early proposal looked beyond that, to a grand Court of Honor, stretching north of the Terminal. Others saw possibilities for including cultural institutions such as the Metropolitan Opera, a new Madison Square Garden, or a new National Academy of Design. Ultimately, even though Wilgus had long since left the scene, his financial and commercial approach prevailed, with hotels and office buildings surrounding the Terminal and apartment buildings lining Park Avenue.

14 Grand Central Terminal, the great crossroads at the heart of midtown transit.

Vanderbilt Avenue

The New York Central rebuilt Vanderbilt Avenue with hotels, a club, and offices—all masonry buildings designed in generally neoclassical styles to match the Terminal. A 1980s alteration to the Biltmore Hotel, between 43rd and 44th streets, converted it into an office building faced in glass and granite, but the Yale Club and Roosevelt Hotel still mirror the Terminal's style, helping Vanderbilt Avenue maintain more of the original flavor of Terminal City than any other section.

The Biltmore Hotel

"This notion of a hotel built in connection with a terminal provides endless diversion for the idle fancy…. Your business man from Chicago will be able to … go directly from the train to his rooms … dine in the big dining hall, revel in a Turkish bath and spacious plunge there that night, travel on down to one of those big office buildings that have Subway connections in their basements, wind up his business, and return by the Subway to his hotel, to his train, and to Chicago without ever having put his head out of doors in New York."
—*NEW YORK TIMES*, FEBRUARY 2, 1913

"In architectural beauty, interior adornment, and arrangement for the comfort and convenience

of its guests, the Biltmore is unusual. Externally it is … a modern adaptation of the architecture of the Italian Renaissance, and in general outline and color it harmonizes with the Grand Central Terminal, of which it may be considered a supplemental part."
—*NEW YORK TIMES*, DECEMBER 26, 1913

"Under the Biltmore Clock … For college students coming to New York for a weekend, the Biltmore Hotel has always been 'the' place to meet because it is popular, respectable and conveniently located just across from the Grand Central Station. But an even greater lure is that if the collegians don't have a date when they arrive, they usually have no trouble at all finding one 'under the clock' in the Biltmore lobby."
—*LIFE*, APRIL 21, 1952

15 The clock at the Biltmore Hotel. Life, *April 21, 1952.* *Photograph by Ralph Morse. Time Life Pictures/Getty Images*

16 The Biltmore Hotel, seen from the elevated roadway on the west side of the Terminal, 1914. The Biltmore figured from the first as part of Wilgus's plan. Designed by Warren & Wetmore in conjunction with the Terminal, located directly above the incoming station, it included connecting elevators and passageways. Many European train stations included hotels within their structures; in New York, the Biltmore comes closest to this model. *Photograph © Bettman/CORBIS*

Yale Club, the Vanderbilt Concourse Building, and the Roosevelt Hotel

Warren & Wetmore created a uniform look for Terminal City simply by designing so many of its buildings. But the firm also kept an eye on plans by other architects. George B. Post modeled the interiors of the Roosevelt Hotel on a series of famous colonial buildings, but in keeping with the style of Terminal City, he designed the hotel's exterior as an Italian Renaissance palace, blown up to skyscraper proportions. Even as grand an institution as the Yale Club, with as prestigious an architect as James Gamble Rogers (Yale Class of 1899), had to submit its plans to Warren & Wetmore for approval, "to make sure," said the *Chicago Daily Tribune*, in January of 1914, "that the new building would not be out of harmony with the Grand Central station, the Biltmore hotel, and other surrounding structures." The Yale Club's restrained neoclassicism nicely matches the neighboring Vanderbilt Concourse Building, which Warren & Wetmore designed in the same year.

17 West side of Vanderbilt Avenue, looking south, past the Roosevelt Hotel , 1935. On the next block stand the Vanderbilt Concourse Building and the Yale Club, with the Biltmore Hotel visible in the distance. *Courtesy of the Museum of the City of New York, Berenice Abbott Collection*

42nd Street and Lexington Avenue

While the Vanderbilt Avenue buildings stood across the street from the Terminal, linked to it only below ground, buildings on 42nd Street and Lexington Avenue shared a closer physical connection, with direct street-level contact: the Commodore Hotel on 42nd Street, filling the block between Depew Place and Lexington Avenue; the Graybar Building abutting the Commodore on Lexington; and, next to the Graybar, a new post office—a logical location, as in those years the mail traveled by rail. The Graybar itself replaced the Grand Central Palace, an enormous exhibition hall.

Warren & Wetmore designed both the Commodore and the post office. They also designed a new Grand Central Palace a few blocks to the north of the original. The Palace has long since been demolished; a complete renovation of the Commodore, now called the Grand Hyatt, reclad its somber masonry in mirror glass; and a new tower now rises above the post office, but the Graybar Building survives largely intact, and thoroughly integrated with the Terminal.

The Commodore Hotel

"One of the most important features of the Commodore Hotel, designed to be the largest hostelry in the world, will be the ease with which the guests, numbering many hundred thousands each year, will be able to travel from the hotel to various parts of the city."
—*NEW-YORK TRIBUNE*, MAY 20, 1917

"A group of representative New Yorkers stood in the lobby of the new Hotel Commodore on the night that it was opened.... Presently a man in the group, a banker of international prominence, exclaimed, 'It is wonderful! It is the very last word in modern civilization!'"
—*ARCHITECTURE AND BUILDING*, APRIL 1919

18 The Commodore Hotel, honoring the memory of Commodore Vanderbilt, is seen here in 1919, prior to the demolition of the Third Avenue Elevated spur. Warren & Wetmore's staid neoclassical masonry facade let the hotel stand as a quiet but supportive visual neighbor to the Terminal.

The Graybar Building

19 The thirty-two-story Graybar Building on Lexington Avenue; Sloan & Robertson, architects, 1927. Originally home to the Graybar Electric Company, a Western Electric subsidiary. The building connects directly to the Terminal via the "Graybar Passage." *Courtesy of the Museum of the City of New York, Wurts Bros. Collection*

20, 22 Details over the entrance to the Graybar Passage, including six Assyrian-style reliefs representing air, fire, water, earth, transportation, and communication. According to architect John Sloan, as quoted in the *New Yorker* in 1933,

the firm chose the Assyrian style because "the building is owned by Eastern Offices, Incorporated. We thought it would be appropriate to decorate it in the Eastern manner." *Photographs by David Thompson (reliefs, 2011; baffled rats, 2008)*

21 Vault in the Graybar Passage painted by Edward Trumbull, 1927. The central mural has been restored, but extensions to either side had deteriorated beyond rescue, 1984. *Photograph by Frank English*

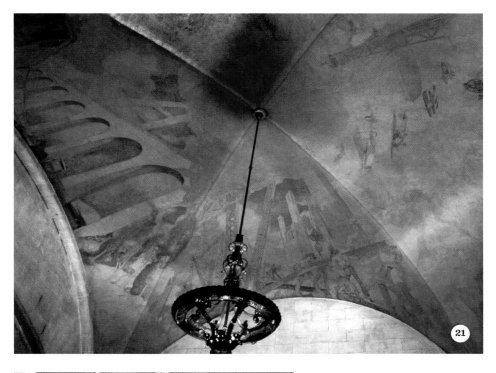

"On the west side of the vault ... will be depicted a train drawn by a giant electric locomotive passing beneath a bridge. The painting, including such details as electric signals, is intended to picture the advance made in railroading by the use of electricity. On the east side ... control of the air will be symbolized in portrayals of airplanes and radio instruments. A large airship will be shown gliding out of a cloud. Such twentieth century devices as the telephone and telegraph also will be shown. The north side will represent the erection of steel work in a large skyscraper.... A Bessemer converter will indicate the processes used in modern manufacture of steel."

—*NEW YORK TIMES*, MARCH 20, 1927

"Up each of [the struts supporting the marquee] is climbing a big iron rat, which, however, is prevented from entering the building by one of those inverted, funnel-shaped guards known to seafaring folk, we find, as 'bafflers.' They are put on ships' hawsers to keep rats from climbing up...."

—*NEW YORKER*, SEPTEMBER 9, 1933

Grand Central Post Office

23 The United States Postal Service came to rely on trains to carry the mail—hence the post office opposite Penn Station and the one adjoining Grand Central Terminal. Reed & Stem and Warren & Wetmore designed the new post office at Lexington Avenue and 45th Street while planning the design of the Terminal, and it matches the complex's overall architectural style. In 1915 the post office expanded into a second building just to its north. *Courtesy of the Science, Industry & Business Library, The New York Public Library, Astor, Lenox, and Tilden Foundations*

Grand Central Palace

"The new Grand Central Palace, next to the Grand Central Depot, is to be fully thrown open to the public for the first time to inaugurate the Press Club Fair. It is probably the largest exposition building in the United States outside of the Chicago Fair Grounds, and contains over 240,000 square feet of actual floor space (over three times greater than Madison Square Garden).... In interior beauty and comfort, and in light (which by day is supplied through a marvelous glass dome, and by night through thousands upon thousands of electric lights) the building has no equal in New York."

—*SOUVENIR AND OFFICIAL PROGRAMME OF THE PRESS CLUB FAIR: GRAND CENTRAL PALACE,* MAY 1893

"New York's future great show house, the New Grand Central Palace, now approaching completion, has thirteen stories, occupies an entire city block, and will have a floor space of over 600,000 square feet.... The new exposition building will, for the purposes of show promoters, solve the problem of housing the great exhibitions peculiar to the metropolis.... The New Grand Central Palace is an important phase of the grand architectural, engineering, and municipal improvement plan of the New York Central and Hudson River Railroad's magnificent metropolitan terminal."

—*WASHINGTON POST,* FEBRUARY 12, 1911

24 A new and larger Grand Central Palace—designed by Reed & Stem and Warren & Wetmore, and built in 1911 on the west side of Lexington between 46th and 47th streets—became the first new building of Terminal City. Both Palaces housed enormous trade shows, especially exhibitions of automobiles and flowers. The second Grand Central Palace was demolished in 1964. *Photograph by A. E. French/Getty Images*

25 The original Grand Central Palace opened in 1893 on the west side of Lexington Avenue at 43rd Street, on the site of today's Graybar Building; it was demolished to make way for the Terminal. *Illustration from the Souvenir and Offical Programme of the Press Club Fair, May 5, 1893.*

Park Avenue

North of the Terminal, straddling Park Avenue, the New York Central Building turns its face to the north, much as the Terminal looks south. The building once closed a vista of a broad, landscaped avenue lined with neoclassical masonry apartment houses, many of them designed by Warren & Wetmore. As elsewhere in Terminal City, even the buildings designed by other firms deliberately tried to match the overall style set by the Terminal's architects. A second wave of development following World War II replaced most of Park Avenue's buildings with steel and glass skyscrapers, leaving just a few older buildings as a reminder of the original Terminal City.

New York Central Building

"Gold is a conspicuous note in the decoration inside.... Mr. Whitney Warren, the architect, believed a great railway building should have warmth and richness. The lobby gleams with cornices and friezes of gold, and several varieties of colored marble.... Mr. Warren is particularly proud of the elevators.... There are forty of them— with red walls and a blue cloudy ceiling and a great deal of bright gold trimming."
—*NEW YORKER*, FEBRUARY 9, 1929

"On the left is Transportation, symbolized by a male figure who bears a general resemblance to our old friend Mercury. His mate, a graceful woman, carries the attribute of Industry, the distaff, while her arm, with a certain recklessness, embraces a beehive. The design is instinct with the elegance of style for which McCartan is famous: a style derived from the French, and consequently admirably suited to the spirit of the detail with which Warren & Wetmore have enriched these high portals."
—*NEW YORKER*, DECEMBER 15, 1928

26 The lobby of the New York Central Building is a north–south corridor connecting 45th and 46th streets; the round arches on either side lead to smaller elevator vestibules, 2012. *Photograph by Frank English*

27 Figures, designed by Edward McCartan, flanking the clock over the 46th Street entrance to the New York Central Building. Though not nearly so large, they reflect the Coutan sculpture and Tiffany clock over Grand Central's 42nd Street entrance. *Photograph by Wurts Bros. Courtesy of Milstein Division of United States History. Local History & Genealogy, The New York Public Library, Astor, Lenox and Tilden Foundations.*

"Park Avenue development within the last six years constitutes one of the most striking chapters in the real estate history of New York. The transformation of this broad highway, resting on the tracks of the New York Central railroad, from a lane of old flats and tumble-down nondescript buildings of various types within the last decade, into a leading residential community ranking with Fifth Avenue, records one of the most remarkable architectural triumphs in the annals of the city.... After completion of the New York Central's terminal work, which gave Park Avenue three new blocks from Forty-fifth to Fiftieth Street, the old brewery had stood as an obstacle.... Today, the classic new edifice of St. Bartholomew's Church ... attests to the revolutionary change in the district."

—*NEW YORK TIMES*, JUNE 26, 1921

"Traffic will pass directly through a skyscraper in a unique project now under construction in the very heart of New York City. One of the principal highways of the city, leading to a great railroad terminal, the Grand Central Station, is to pierce the thirty-two-story structure with twin tunnels. When the work is finished, you will be able to drive into the building at street level, climb through it on an inclined roadway, and emerge at the other side on an outdoor elevated roadway that circles the station itself at a height of one story above the street."

—*POPULAR SCIENCE*, APRIL 1928

28 Park Avenue looking north before the widening of the avenue in 1927. Though the City renamed Fourth Avenue as Park Avenue in the nineteenth century, only with the Terminal City redevelopment did it come to earn that name. St. Bartholomew's church, on the right, replaced the old Schaefer brewery. Architect Bertram Goodhue incorporated into his Byzantine-style church a porch designed by McKim, Mead & White for St. Bart's former home as a memorial to Cornelius Vanderbilt II—a gift from the Vanderbilt family that the congregation felt obliged to bring along to the new site. The church is the only building in the photo still standing, 1922. *Courtesy of the Museum of the City of New York, Byron Co. Collection*

29 Cars entering and leaving the New York Central Building's tunnels connecting to the elevated viaduct around the Terminal, 1933. *Courtesy NYC Municipal Archives, Borough President Manhattan Collection*

30 New York Central Building, looking south along the Park Avenue divider, 1929.

"Everybody knows about the difficulty of building buildings over the Central's tracks—how one apartment house vibrated distressingly for years until it was discovered that one little rivet in a pillar in the basement came in contact with metal connected with the tracks; and everybody knows how all the buildings in that region now are built with a two-inch space between the base of their walls and the sidewalks, because the sidewalks are supported by steel pillars springing from the track area and might transmit shivers all through the structures."

—*NEW YORKER*, FEBRUARY 9, 1929

31 The Waldorf-Astoria, designed by Schultze & Weaver, built 1929–1931, was the last and largest hotel erected in Terminal City. Leonard Schultze, formerly on the staff of Warren & Wetmore, had played a role in the design of Grand Central. The original Waldorf made way for the Empire State Building. The new Waldorf's twin towers dominated Park Avenue, and signaled the eventual coming of a second wave of development, starting in the early 1950s, that would line the avenue with skyscrapers. The Waldorf-Astoria and St. Bartholomew's church are two of the last survivors of the pre–World War II Park Avenue north of the Terminal, the only others being the Racquet Club and the Postum Building.

31

2. Grand Central Terminal.
4. Hotel Commodore.
5. Graybar Building.
6. Post Office, G.C.T. Branch.
7. 466 Lexington Avenue Building.
31. Hotel Biltmore.
32. Vanderbilt Avenue Building.
33. Hotel Belmont.
35. Murray Hill Hotel.
44. The Gilford.
45. New York Library.

1. New York Central Building.
8. Grand Central Palace.
9. Park - Lexington Building.
10. 277 Park Avenue.
11. The Barclay.
12. The Park Lane.
23. 290 Park Avenue.
24. 270 Park Avenue.
25. Postum Building.
26. 385 Madison Avenue.
27. 379 Madison Avenue.
28. Hotel Roosevelt.
30. Yale Club.
38. Lorraine Hotel.
39. Ritz-Carlton Hotel.
42. Shelton Hotel.
43. The Winthrop.

32

"**The Commodore, the Roosevelt, the Postum and Catts Buildings, the Grand Central Palace, the monstrous Graybar Building just completed, countless apartment houses, one by one have perched themselves over the railway tracks. Any real estate man can trace the area for you on a map.**"
—*NEW YORKER*, JANUARY 1, 1927

32 Map of the Terminal Zone in a promotional brochure for the New York Central Building, c. 1928.

33 Lever House, Park Avenue and 54th Street, built in 1952 to designs by Gordon Bunshaft of Skidmore, Owings & Merrill. *Courtesy of the Museum of the City of New York, Wurts Bros. Collection*

34 Seagram Building, Park Avenue and 53rd Street, built in 1958 to designs by Mies van der Rohe. These two steel and glass International Style skyscrapers, among the first in the country, led to the rebuilding of Park Avenue in similar style, as far north as 59th Street.
Photograph by Tom Ravenscroft

35 Map of the Terminal Zone from a promotional brochure for the "Eastern Offices" building, c. 1927 (before it had been renamed the Graybar Building).

36 Park Avenue, looking south to the New York Central Building, with the Pan Am (now MetLife) Building behind it. Where once the masonry-clad New York Central Building closed the Park Avenue vista of masonry apartment buildings, now the glassy skyscraper rising behind it closes the vista of tall glass office buildings. Though almost nothing of its earlier self survives, today's Park Avenue owes its entire development—and the steel structure underpinning it—to the Terminal's visionary planners of a century ago.

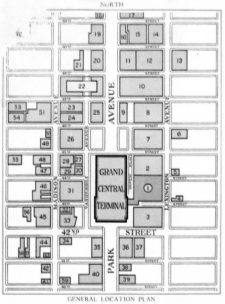

LIST OF BUILDINGS

35

GENERAL LOCATION PLAN

PAN AM

5

BEHIND THE SCENES

Perhaps the most remarkable aspect of the experience of arriving at or leaving from Grand Central is how simple it seems to be—and how complex it actually is.

Inside the Terminal, travelers can enter the Concourse, check the clock, scan the announcement board, ask for information, buy a ticket, find a gate, and board a train in a matter of minutes. Yet from beginning to end, that process is guided across a vast infrastructure tended by an expert staff. The clock must be accurate, the information correct and easy to find, and tickets easy to purchase.

Outside, in the train shed, each train departs on one of some forty active tracks, on one of two levels, and must then be carefully threaded first onto ten tracks and then onto four tracks, without colliding with other trains. All trains roll northward underground, in century-old tunnels beneath Park Avenue and the buildings that line it, for two and a half miles, under the watchful eye of rail traffic controllers who track each train's every move with the latest computer technology.

1   Brakeman hauling equipment during
     restoration of Park Avenue tunnel, 1989.
     Photo by Frank English

MECCA *for* MILLIONS

LONG MAY IT WAVE

BUY MORE WAR BONDS

SERVICE MEN'S LOUNGE

COACH TICKETS NO RESERVATIONS

2

Inside the Terminal

The Crowds

"In addition to its more than 100,000 railroad passengers a day, at least three times that many more persons go through some part of the terminal. In the center of what is perhaps as densely populated a spot as any in the city except the financial district in peak prosperity, it affords weatherproof passage."

—*NEW YORK TIMES*, JANUARY 30, 1938

2   Use of Terminal reaches a peak during the war era. *Courtesy* of Popular Mechanics. *Originally published in the November 1944 issue.*

3   Jacob "Jake the Clock Man" Bachtold, clock master for New York Central, checking the clock in the incoming station, now the Biltmore Room, against his watch, c. 1950. The clock master is responsible for maintaining and cleaning all the clocks throughout the Terminal.

Keeping Time

"Conductors, trainmen, and others are compelled to keep their watches in strict conformity with the superintendent's clock.... The time is distributed over the line each week day as follows: At 10 o'clock 58 minutes and 30 seconds A.M. the word 'time' is sent by the main office to the telegraph stations between New York and Albany. The word is repeated for 28 seconds, during which time operators must see that their instruments are adjusted. At 10 o'clock and 50 minutes [the] seconds commence beating and continue for 50 seconds. The word 'switch' is then sent over the wire, and operators having electric clocks connect them immediately with the circuit known as No. 9 wire. Ten seconds are allowed in which to make the connection. At 11 A.M., with one touch of the New York key, the hands of the different clocks are set to 11 o'clock. If they are fast or slow they change at once to the hour named."

—*RAILWAY WORLD*, AUGUST 7, 1880

"Jacob Bachtold, who is in charge of time in this vicinity for the New York Central ... superintends a thousand clocks.... In regulating all clocks, [Bachtold] depends on a twenty-year-old Hamilton watch ... [He] checks this every morning with a master clock in the train dispatcher's office, which is checked twice a day with the Naval Observatory in Washington. ... Eventually, after worrying over twelve time clocks used daily by Central employees, he gets around to the grandfather's clock in the office of Frederick E. Williamson, president of the railroad, on the thirty-second floor of the Park Avenue building."

—*NEW YORKER*, APRIL 27, 1940

"The four-faced 'Golden Clock' above the information booth in the middle of the main concourse of Grand Central Terminal will be removed for repairs next Tuesday. That will be the first interruption to the bronze clock's ticking in the 21,500,000 minutes, more or less, since the terminal was opened in 1913. A spokesman ... admitted yesterday that the ... timepiece was losing a 'minute or two per day.' The error was corrected hourly, however, by the electric control system tied to the Naval Observatory."
—*NEW YORK TIMES*, JANUARY 17, 1954

"One of Jake's most important clocks is the one on the south side of Grand Central.... its hands weigh over a hundred pounds each ... [but] are so nearly perfectly balanced that they can be moved by a little wheel in the works, which are inside the building. Occasionally, Bachtold has to do something to the face of this clock, in which event he emerges through a door about three feet square at numeral VI and works either sitting on the doorway or standing on the stone coping beneath the clock, in either case appreciably slowing down northbound motor traffic.... [He] regards clocks as personalities and can tell in advance how they'll go wrong.... Clocks have been his life since, as a boy, he was apprenticed to a clockmaker in Switzerland, where he was born. He's sixty-three now, and estimates that he has walked thirty thousand miles inspecting clocks since he went to work for the Central, in 1903. He had only fifty clocks to look after then. Twenty of these are still in use."
—*NEW YORKER*, APRIL 27, 1940

" 'Whatever time I give them, that's the time the railroad runs on,' [the 61-year-old Mr. Kugler] said. 'Imagine if one day I decided to set things just a minute late....' Each Grand Central Clock has two hands and is operated by batteries that wind up a spring that in turn drives the clock mechanically.... Nearly all [the clocks] are connected to the 'master clock' in Mr. Kugler's workshop, an instrument that keeps the rest of them in line. The master clock sends out impulses that can correct errant clocks up to two minutes each hour."
—*NEW YORK TIMES*, APRIL 25, 1980

The Information Booth

"One of the most marvelous products of the present age is the man, or group of men, in the 'Information Bureau' at a great railway terminal. He is distinctly a product of this age of rush and congestion and specialization.... His head is a psychologic [sic] marvel, synchronized with the clock and the calendar; automatically he knows 'what's the next train?' whether it be on a full-schedule weekday, or a slim-schedule Sunday or holiday. His ready-reference memory for minutely exact facts and figures goes a long way toward confuting the doctrine of human fallibility. And his double-weave, seamless, never-rip patience would bring a tinge of green into the eyes of Job himself.

'Information men' deal largely with time tables, and time tables deal almost exclusively with figures.... Now, if you will take the total number of trains ... and multiply them by the number of stations, the result will represent a small part of the exact-to-the-minute facts that must be photographed upon the memory of the 'information man.' Between the Grand Central and Albany, Chatham and New Haven are branch lines, and beyond Albany, Chatham and New Haven are trunk lines, with their own particular branch lines. All of these lines mean stations, and all of these stations mean more figures for the 'information man.'"

—*NEW YORK TIMES*, JUNE 11, 1916

6

4 The exterior of the Tiffany clock is reached through the door at numeral VI. *Courtesy of the* New York Times

5 Clock master Paul Kugler at work on the "Golden Clock" in 1978. Like his predecessor, Jake Bachtold, Kugler believed that "all clocks have personalities. Some are constant trouble-makers and some just have a bad day." *Courtesy of Michael Vitiello, Williamson Library*

6 The "Golden Clock" above the Information Booth. The Self Winding Clock Company manufactured many of the Terminal's clocks, and then turned over installation and maintenance to Western Union, which synchronized them with its own master clock, whose time depended on the U.S. Naval Observatory in Washington, D.C.

"Don't just sit there doing nothing! Ask each other questions." *(7)*

"Mr. Bradley, today's guest expert from the B. & O., will answer that one." *(8)*

"What time do you play 'Baby, It's Cold Outside'?" *(9)*

"Stop saying, 'I'm glad you asked that question,' Harris. Just give the answers." *(10)*

7–10 *Courtesy of the* New Yorker.

7: Cartoon by Alain, November 26, 1955 issue; 8: Cartoon by Richard Decker, May 18, 1940 issue; 9: Cartoon by Frank Modell, December 24, 1949 issue; 10: Cartoon by Frank Modell, August 27, 1955 issue

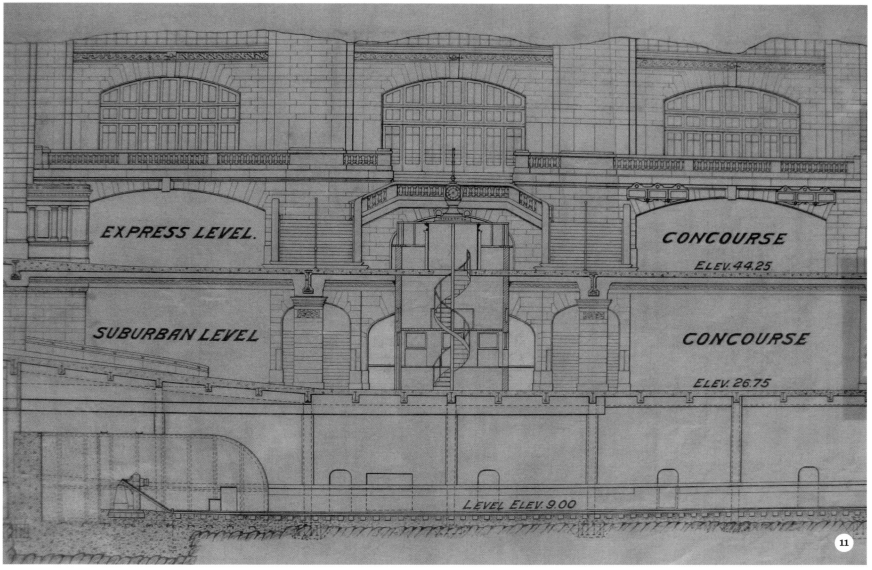

EXPRESS LEVEL.

CONCOURSE

ELEV. 44.25

SUBURBAN LEVEL

CONCOURSE

ELEV. 26.75

LEVEL ELEV. 9.00

11

"Sometimes the clerks at the information booth at the Grand Central station wonder themselves why they don't go mad. Folks ask the silliest questions. 'Where could I have a live turkey stored until Christmas?' 'I'm going to Chicago the day before Christmas. Will the train get there in time?' 'Can I take a kitchen table and four chairs with me on the train and put them under my berth?' 'Can you tell me the address of a lady who came here three years ago from Czecho-Slovakia and married a banker in Westchester? The banker died, and I can't recall his name.' ... These, explained W.P. Walsh, in charge of the Grand Central information service, are some of the reasons why it requires about three years to train a good information man [to handle] the 25,000 questions the bureau is called upon to answer each day."

—*ATLANTA CONSTITUTION*, DECEMBER 22, 1930

12

11 A drawing from 1916, showing the spiral staircase inside the Information Booth that connects to the booth on the lower level.

12 *Photograph by Frank English, 1988*

"Grand Central is replacing its old-fashioned train-arrival blackboard with an electric billboard. The sign, which will eliminate a trainman writing in a bold script with a piece of chalk on the board, is being erected on the top of the ticket booths in the grand concourse. Lester Onderdonk, a 58-year-old railroad employe [*sic*] from Hastings-On-Hudson, was disenchanted. He put down his piece of chalk at his post at the old train-arrivals board in the small waiting room under Vanderbilt Avenue, shut off his microphone for the public-address system that announced trains and where lost people can meet and said: 'Do you know what I hope? I hope that when they plug in the new system, when it is finished in a week or two, the whole thing blows up.'"

—*NEW YORK TIMES*, JANUARY 13, 1967

13 Until 1967, a railroad attendant updated time and track information for arriving trains on a chalkboard in the Biltmore Room. *Courtesy of the Harry Ransom Center, the University of Texas at Austin*

14 For several years, Grand Central used a "split-flap" display board of the type manufactured in Italy by Solari di Udine. The Grand Central board was made by the American Sign & Indicator Corporation in Spokane, Washington, in association with Solari. *Photograph by Frank English, 1985*

15 Reservation Bureau, *Reprinted from* Central Headlight, *June 1945*

Reservation Bureau

"Redecoration of the New York Central Pullman Reservation Bureau, Grand Central Terminal, included soundproofing and air-conditioning, both of which were made necessary by the steady increase of personnel. Because of wartime passenger traffic, the personnel has grown from approximately 60 in 1940 to 159. Photo ... shows the rows of sliding diagram racks operated by seated reservation clerks, with supervisors standing at call to solve problems."

—*CENTRAL HEADLIGHT*, JUNE 1945

Baggage Handlers

"The [baggage] checking arrangement is typical of the conveniences installed. The traveler will not have to go to the baggage room. All he will have to do is to present his railroad ticket and transfer claim check at the checking stand. He will receive in exchange for his claim check a baggage check, the claim check being sent by pneumatic tube to the baggage room to identify the piece to be checked.... Outgoing baggage is loaded on electric trucks and sent down by elevators to the baggage subway. The trucks are then sent through the subway and lifted by elevators to the track level. The baggage is then transferred to the designated train. The operation is reversed for the incoming trains. By this arrangement the passenger platforms are kept free of baggage trucks, a nuisance ordinarily encountered in railroad stations."

—*RAILWAY AND ENGINEERING REVIEW*, JANUARY 25, 1913

"Subways for the handling of baggage, mail and express below the lower level are at the lowest elevation of any of the terminal passageways, being between 50 and 60 ft. below the level of the street.... Here all of the baggage, mail and express received and sent out of the terminal is transferred to and from the individual tracks of the upper and lower levels by means of elevators connecting with the subways, so that there is a minimum of baggage trucking on the train platforms."

—*ENGINEERING NEWS-RECORD*, SEPTEMBER 9, 1920

16 Baggage claim area, c. 1930.

17 Looking south toward the 45th Street facade of the baggage building (now site of the Met Life Building) at the rear of Grand Central Terminal, circa 1916, prior to construction of the New York Central Building that straddles Park Avenue between 45th and 46th streets.

HAND BAGGAGE DELIVERED

LOST PROPERTY ROOM

NOTICE TO THE PUBLIC:
AGGAGE MUST BE EXAMINED WHEN DELIVERED TO PARTY PRESENTING CLAIM CHECK
NLESS DAMAGE TO BAGGAGE OR CONTENTS IS THEN NOTED. CLAIMS FOR
LLEGED DAMAGE SUBSEQUENTLY PRESENTED WILL NOT BE RECOGNIZED.

18

Lost and Found

"Richard Butler, head of [the Lost and Found Department], is so used to strange articles that he experiences little emotion on receiving a kitten, turtle, marriage license, or a wooden leg…. Every day there flows into the Lost and Found Department a stream of men, women and children, persons of all classes, rich and poor, educated and uneducated, plain, handsome and middling—in short a cross-section of America…. Some of them approach the desk sheepishly. Others are excited and come almost on a run, but practically all of them are reasonable and express warm appreciation of the valuable service that this department provides…. Butler even has some regular customers. One man … was in the habit of bringing in a lunch of crackers and jelly. Regularly, at least once a week, he would leave his lunch on the train, to retrieve it later from Butler. Another Mr. Forgetful has left his suitcase, pipe, razor, phonograph records, umbrella and packages he was taking home to his wife. These last always gave him more concern than did any of the others. Every married man will understand why."
—*NEW YORK TIMES*, SEPTEMBER 19, 1920

"Sooner or later, one of almost everything shows up at Grand Central Terminal lost and found…. Travelers who come in to look for eyeglasses are handed a heavy drawerful to squint at. Separate drawers are crammed with checkbooks, address books, wristwatches and jewelry. Winter accessories are somewhat more systematized; empty cardboard cartons borrowed from the liquor store next door are labelled 'Hats, Feb. '78,' or 'Gloves, March '78.' Belts and ties are similarly sorted."
—*NEW YORK TIMES*, APRIL 4, 1978

18 Lost Property Room, 1936. As of 1920, some fifteen thousand to eighteen thousand lost items found their way every year to Grand Central's "Lost and Found Department."

"A child's stuffed animal. A pair of socks. A coffee mug. They are the casualties of the daily bustle of New York's Grand Central Terminal…. Normally, these unclaimed items would just accumulate at a lost-and-found office at Grand Central, the city's giant railway station. But for the next month, they have been elevated to the world of art. 'Lost property,' a 'living art' exhibit of the misplaced belongings of train commuters, opened May 11 at the terminal. It is one of four Manhattan creations entitled 'LOST: New York Projects,' by French conceptual artist Christian Boltanski."

—*CHRISTIAN SCIENCE MONITOR*, MAY 19, 1995

"In a typical year about 3,000 coats and jackets; 2,500 cellphones; 2,000 sets of keys; 1,500 wallets, purses and ID's; and 1,100 umbrellas find their way into the Metro-North Lost and Found in Grand Central Terminal. That, along with some stranger items like a basset hound, $9,999 in cash stuffed into a pair of socks … two sets of false teeth and a $10,000 diamond ring, makes the task of sorting and returning as much as possible a formidable one…. In 1990 … only about a quarter of the 400 or so items the center received in a month were returned to their owners. In May of this year, 1,700 items were turned in and more than 900 were returned. The sharp increase … is due in large part to [computerizing] the operation."

—*NEW YORK TIMES*, AUGUST 20, 2002

19 Christian Boltanski. *New York Projects: Lost Property, Grand Central Terminal,* 1995, *Photograph by Dorothy Zeidman. Courtesy of the Public Art Fund, Marian Goodman Gallery, New York*

20, 21 Today's Lost and Found office, 2008. *Photographs by Patrick Cashin*

Stationmaster's Office

As the title suggests, the stationmaster's responsibilities extend to most things that happen inside the Terminal. The stationmaster's staff of 160—which includes the building's custodians—focuses on customer service: making sure passengers get to the right train in the event of a track change, helping with luggage, providing wheelchairs, even comforting troubled passengers. They act as the Terminal's foot soldiers, checking that trains are on time and passengers are in the right place. They also act as an extension of the Information Booth (by far the most frequently asked question: "Where are the bathrooms?"). Over time, the stationmaster's office has moved around the Terminal—from an office under a Vanderbilt Avenue stairway, to an office near the entrance to Track 39, to a converted men's room, to an office perched above the ramp near the Oyster Bar—settling in its current location in 1998 near track 36.

"At Grand Central Terminal, they call him 'Mr. Courtesy.' Among his friends are Red Caps and royalty, campers and commuters, President Eisenhower, Sophie Tucker and Cardinal Spellman. He is Edward George Fischer, the terminal's general station master.... As head of a terminal that handles 5,000,000 passengers each month, Mr. Fischer is in charge of a 700-man work force. He must see that 543 trains get in and out daily, and he must soothe complainers about a variety of malfunctions that range from a lack of hot water on the Twentieth Century Limited [the luxury New York Central train connecting New York and Chicago] to a train that was late. He must be patient and informed when he meets reporters trying to beat a deadline on a holiday travel story, and must be calm with excited people who lose all sorts of items."

—*NEW YORK TIMES*, AUGUST 22, 1958

22 Current stationmaster's office, 2008.
Photograph by Frank English

23

Red Caps

"There were but thirteen tracks running into what is now Grand Central Station, and but ten porters, when George Schuman went to work there, almost half a century ago, at unloading mail and baggage.... 'About the time the station was finished I went over and asked for a job. They needed porters and I got a job at $42.50 a month unloading and loading mail and baggage.... The first uniforms were green and gold. Then they put us into blue blouses and brown corduroy pants. Finally one of the officials of the New York Central brought back twelve red caps from London, so we all put on red caps, the first ones in New York City. I remember that the timetables were marked with the words 'Do not tip the Red Caps.' We got few tips in those days; just our salary.'"

—*NEW YORK TIMES*, JUNE 1, 1924

"Even the humble, red-capped porters, whose chief business is to wait on travelers, are carefully drilled until they can supply readily and courteously all ordinary information about trains. Should they be unable to answer a question, they do not direct the inquirer to some one else; instead, they escort him to one of the attendants in gray frock coats and white caps, who are walking encyclopedias.... In short, personal service is the keynote to which everything in this railroad palace is attuned. While facilities have been provided for handling a quarter of a million persons a day, each one is made to feel that he is the only passenger the New York Central has, and that it is afraid of losing him."

—*RAILWAY AND ENGINEERING REVIEW*, JANUARY 25, 1913

23 A "Red Cap" porter carting luggage for Twentieth Century Limited passengers, in the 1950s. So-called for the color of their headgear, the Red Caps—once numbering more than five hundred—served as porters and baggage handlers at the Terminal.

By FAIRFAX DOWNEY • *Drawing by* JEFFERSON MACHAMER

Some of the last-minute messages which the Green Caps at the Grand Central Station are given to deliver.

24

Green Caps

"Thousands of commuters who passed through the Grand Central Terminal last week noticed a young man in a smart uniform, trimmed with green, and a green cap…. A dozen green caps … will … act as private secretaries for those who need their services. Should a commuter or a traveler from out of town desire to send a message to a friend or business acquaintance, the Green Cap will see that it is telephoned for a small fee. Should the commuter want his wife notified that he will be home earlier or later than usual the Green Cap will oblige. In fact, for a dime the Green Cap will telephone that a commuting husband will not be home at all."

—*NEW YORK TIMES*, JUNE 25, 1922

"Tell your troubles to the Green Cap. If you miss your train; if you are going to be late for dinner; if you forgot your brief case; if you could not get the theater tickets; if the car broke down; give the message to the Green Cap at the Grand Central Terminal and he will make everything all right again, with your wife, your office, your garage…. There was a woman—a nervous, tired little woman—who had waited five hours for her husband to meet her under the clock. She finally discovered the Green Cap message service and laid her troubles before the sympathetic manager. Her husband worked in a lunchroom in Newark. She knew only the street address, not the telephone number. It was too much for her inexperience to locate him, but the Green Caps aren't afraid of 'Information.' They got Friend Husband on the telephone and he promised to dash right over. That was the way things went all day yesterday, the first in the career of the Green Caps."

—*NEW-YORK TRIBUNE*, JULY 2, 1922

24 The "Green Caps," an innovation of 1922, functioned as part of a message exchange service for travelers. The exchange accepted phone messages for travelers or made phone calls to relay messages from them. A dozen Green Caps circulated in the Terminal—at the gates, under the clock, on the floor—making themselves available to the passengers. Two runners collected the messages from the Green Caps and brought them to the main message exchange office on the Vanderbilt Avenue side of the Terminal. Services soon expanded to include parcel delivery outside the Terminal. *Cartoon from the* New-York Tribune, *July 16, 1922, Courtesy of the Library of Congress*

All Aboard

"The indicators provided before each train gate at both levels consist of two-faced signs, which are placed at right angles so as to be visible from all parts of the room and which bear the name or departing time of the train. In addition there are flat indicators which give the time, name and stops of the trains on display curtains in their upper portions, and have a series of drawers below in which the rolled curtains are kept. The devices are easy of operation and are regulated by hand by the gatemen who also adjust the two-faced signs by electrical control."

—*ARCHITECTURE AND BUILDING*, APRIL 1913

"Everything sparkling clean and in order, the Century, pre-heated in winter, pre-cooled in summer, is backed into Grand Central at 4:50 P.M. A 260 foot red carpet weighing half a ton is unrolled down the platform. Two minutes before departure time a signalman ... pulls a series of switch-throwing levers which will give the great train a clear pathway out of the station. Passenger timetables say the Century departs at 6 P.M. The operational timetables used by train crews are more exact. They read 6:01—to allow stragglers time to get aboard."

—*CHICAGO DAILY TRIBUNE*, AUGUST 25, 1957

25 At the gate to Track 28, preparing to board the Twentieth Century Limited. The luxury train, in service from 1920 to 1967, connected New York with Chicago, famously making the 961-mile run in 960 minutes (sixteen hours).

26 Red Caps at work on the platform, rolling out the red carpet for a Twentieth Century Limited train preparing to leave for Chicago. The *Chicago Tribune* called the carpet "symbolic of the train's service," which also included private rooms, observation cars, a library and a barbershop.

27 Mrs. Frank Arthur Vanderlip, Mrs. Alonzo Barton Hepburn, Dr. Alice Gregory, Mrs. Howard Talbott, and Mrs. Norman de R. Whitehouse on board the Twentieth Century Limited, c. 1925. Mrs. Vanderlip and Mrs. de R. Whitehouse were presidents of the New York State Woman Suffrage Association.

Outside the Terminal: Making Tracks in the Train Shed

When Grand Central opened in 1913, its underground train shed sheltered 123 active tracks—all made possible by the adoption of electricity, and made safe by using Wilgus's design for a "third rail." Of these tracks, sixty-seven served trains carrying passengers and mail—numbers 1 through 42 on the upper level for long-distance trains, and numbers 101 through 125 on the lower level for commuter lines. The remaining fifty-six tracks were used for storage, cleaning, and maintenance. "Ladder tracks" cut diagonally across the train shed to create ease of access among the other tracks, and special loop tracks served both levels. Over the years, the numbers have gone up and down with various track rearrangements—and the lower-level loop no longer exists—but on average the upper level used twenty-seven tracks for boarding trains, and twenty-eight shorter tracks for mail and express services, with other tracks used for temporary storage during the assembly of long-distance trains. On the lower level, passengers boarded trains on seventeen tracks, while thirty-six tracks handled train storage and a few others were used for maintenance—but design of the lower level permitted great flexibility, so that passenger-boarding tracks could be used for equipment storage, and vice versa.

28 William Wilgus and Frank Sprague's design for the "third rail" that provided electricity for trains on the New York Central's tracks.

29 Tracks in the train shed, c. 2007. *Photograph by Frank English*

30 One of the loop tracks, which extended south as far as the front of the Terminal at 42nd Street and Park Avenue, passing around the Oyster Bar, 2009. *Photograph by Frank English*

"While the casual sightseer looking out over the yards and the Park Avenue Plaza from the head building sees only the visible development, the interest of railroad men and engineers will attach also to the vast network of tracks, signaling systems, power, heating and communicating lines, subways and ventilating systems that are necessary to serve the group of buildings as a whole and operate the Grand Central as a railroad terminal as well."
—*RAILWAY REVIEW*, FEBRUARY 5, 1921

"It is the loop system which has been decided upon as the one to be installed in the Grand Central Terminal…. Instead of trains coming in, discharging passengers, and backing out in the old cumbersome fashion, they will continue, when empty, around the loop under the southerly front of the station; and then will run over to one side of the station yard, where they will be cleaned and made ready for the next trip."
—*NEW YORK TIMES*, FEBRUARY 2, 1913

"The area occupied by the express level equals 46.4 acres, and the plans provide for 19.5 miles of track. There are 42 tracks on this level, of which 29 are adjacent to platforms, while the total length of these tracks along platforms on this level is 28,850 ft.... Immediately east of the inbound tracks are located 22 stub end outbound tracks, while east of these there are 11 tracks for the loading of baggage, mail and express, and for storage, with three running tracks beyond connecting with the loop. Between the ladders leading to the outgoing tracks and loop tracks, there are two storage yards for equipment, while the third yard for similar purposes is located in the corner near Fiftieth street and Lexington avenue. A total storage capacity of 1,050 cars is secured on this and the lower level."
—*RAILWAY AGE GAZETTE*, NOVEMBER 22, 1912

"Few of the millions who annually go through Grand Central Terminal see all of it because the building was designed to keep 30,000 people at a time moving to and from trains. The trains themselves, during rush hours, glide in or out at the rate of one every minute on its 67 stub tracks, a two-layer network of steel occupying some 48 acres of the most valuable real estate in the world.... Seldom does a visitor get a chance to explore the railroad yard beneath the 722-foot roof of the main station building and the cavern of rock, steel and concrete which leads the road northward underneath Park Avenue."
—*POPULAR MECHANICS*, NOVEMBER 1944

31 An "interlocking" area in the train shed, where tracks cross or join together, controlled by a system of signals, switches, and control equipment, housed in a signal tower and overseen by a tower operator. *Photograh by Frank English, c. 2007*

32 Trains passing at 97th Street, just outside the portal to two-and-a-half miles of Park Avenue tunnels. *Photograph by Frank English, 2006*

The Operations Control Center: No Crossed Signals

"Seventy-nine acres of tracks over which come and go almost a thousand trains a day, all controlled from one central signal and switch tower! To the railroad man that is one of the greatest of the mechanical triumphs that the completion of the New York Grand Central Terminal typifies. This tower is the central nerve point, the brain of the terminal. It gathers under one masterful control the bewildering train movements over the intricate web of tracks that lead into that great station. Not a wheel can start to turn without the consent of that nerve centre. Not an incoming train, with its precious human load, can enter on its final approach to the platform until the terminal brain has signified its permission."

—*NEW YORK TIMES*, FEBRUARY 2, 1913

The old Grand Central Depot relied on one dispatcher to coordinate traffic into and out of the Depot. The Terminal, far more complex in its operations—with a train yard two city blocks wide, stretching from Lexington Avenue almost to Madison and as far north as 48th Street—originally used five main stations or signal towers, labeled A, B, C, F, and U (several of these made use of substations labeled N, P, R, S, V, W, X, Y, and Z). Tower U, underneath Park Avenue and 59th Street, controlled traffic moving between the four-track section north of 58th Street and the ten-track section to its south. Ten blocks below Tower U, at 49th Street, just south of the point where the ten-track section fans out into the full train shed, a four-story-tall underground signal tower controlled movement within the shed—the upper two stories on the express level called Tower A and the lower two stories on the commuter level called Tower B. One block farther south, at 48th Street, Tower C

controlled traffic in the train yard's storage area, while Tower F controlled traffic on the loops.

Towers A and B each housed an extraordinarily complex "interlocking machine" with levers connected directly to each of the switches in the train shed. The interlocking system remained in place until 1986, when a disastrous fire destroyed Tower B. By 1993, the system had been completely computerized. Today the signaling operations take place in the Operations Control Center on an upper floor in the Terminal. Dispatchers have been replaced by rail traffic controllers, under the supervision of the chief rail traffic controller. Track platform changes must be approved by the yardmaster. One signaling structure is still in use in the train shed, however: the Track 25 office, whose superintendent can override the yardmaster's track choice when necessary.

33 Tower A, 1939. The interlocking machine is so called because all of the levers physically interlock with one another, making a dangerous track and switching configuration impossible.

34 The dispatcher's office at Grand Central Depot, as illustrated in *Scientific American*, December 25, 1875.

Fig 2

BLOCK
CLEAR
UP LINE

Grand Central Depot: 1875

"Three great railroads have their terminal in the Grand Central Depot.... One hundred and eighteen regular, and from ten to fifteen extra, trains daily pass, in one direction or the other over the tracks on the underground road.... Barely two minutes sometimes intervenes between the departure of one train and the incoming of another, and three trains often start at intervals of five minutes apart. It is obvious that, in order to prevent confusion and accidents, the movements of each and every one of these trains ... must be governed with absolute certainty."

—*SCIENTIFIC AMERICAN*, DECEMBER 25, 1875

"Located far up on the north wall of the depot, the view from its broad window extending over the intricate network of rails ... is a small cabin, the interior appearance of which the reader has before him.... On the wall hang signal indicators and bells, time tables, and a huge clock. On the table before the single occupant are a telegraph instrument, a record book, and three rows of ivory buttons, twenty in all. This is the dispatcher's office, and here, by pressing the buttons or manipulating the telegraph key, he controls the movement of every train going or coming, the buttons, through simple electric bells, governing everything near and about the depot, the key transmitting instructions to far off points."

—*SCIENTIFIC AMERICAN*, DECEMBER 25, 1875

Grand Central Terminal: The Interlocking System, 1913–1986

"Herman Offerman has a tough job. As General Yard Master of New York City's Grand Central Terminal, Mr. Offerman is in complete charge of the 32 miles of track, covering 890 acres, within the station yard itself. More than 500 trains, carrying an average of 100,000 people, pass in and out of Grand Central daily. It is Offerman's responsibility to see that the movements of these trains run with clock-like precision. Mr. Offerman has his headquarters, surrounded by tracks, in the switching station below the street level. From there, with the aid of electric charts, he directs the complicated workings of the station yard, keeping in touch with each train that enters or leaves the terminal. A large crew of men working under him does the mechanical work of switching the trains.... At 30, [Offerman] began working in the station yard, but *he was 41 before he had had enough experience to take over the large responsibilities of Yard Master.*"

—*PITTSBURGH PRESS*, MARCH 4, 1938

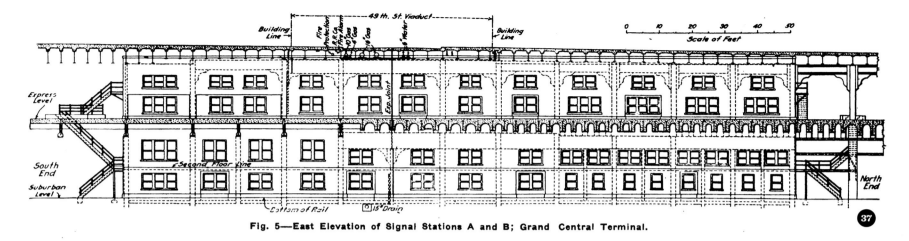

Fig. 5—East Elevation of Signal Stations A and B; Grand Central Terminal.

"The buildings which house main signal stations, A and B, are used not only for the control of the switches and signals but for other purposes also … namely, trainmaster's office; yardmaster's office; office of the foremen of car cleaning and car repairs; foremen of electrical equipment; rest room for enginemen and their assistants; rest room for conductors and trainmen; rooms for track repair men."

—*RAILWAY AGE GAZETTE*, OCTOBER 7, 1910

"As trains pass each tower in turn, the towermen report their direction, time-table number, engine number, track and exact moment of passing, and these data are recorded on special forms known as 'train-sheets' and collected by the dispatchers. The net result is a complete, up-to-the-minute list of all trains on the track and their locations. The dispatchers, completely aware of all the factors involved, plot the schedules and order the movements of trains. The towermen, by operating the levers controlling the switches, and thereby the tracks, supply the routes. The signals, interlocked with the position of the switches, guide the engine drivers."

—*NEW YORK TIMES*, SEPTEMBER 10, 1939

"To operate the complicated network of trackage it was necessary to devise a signaling system for each level that could be operated by a director who could not possibly see the train movements…. Each level is controlled by a director who has before him a facsimile diagram of the track layout on which movement of trains between switches and fouling points is indicated by small electric lights. The signal machine for the suburban level is the largest ever constructed and has 400 levers, each of which operates a switch or signal, and on the floor above, the machine for the upper level has 362 levers."

—*ENGINEERING NEWS-RECORD*, SEPTEMBER 9, 1920

35   Tower U, below Park Avenue at 59th Street, guiding trains into and out of the train shed at the entrance to the Park Avenue Tunnel, in 1911. *Courtesy of Grand Central Collection, Archives Center, National Museum of American History, Smithsonian Institution*

36   Tower A, which housed the hundreds of interlocking levers controlling the express track, in 1911. Not visible is Tower B—located on the lower level directly below Tower A—which housed the interlocking levers for commuter trains. Each lever on the interlocking machines had a unique number, which corresponded with the number on the track switch or signal that it controlled electronically. *Courtesy of Grand Central Collection, Archives Center, National Museum of American History, Smithsonian Institution*

37   "East Elevation of Signal Stations A and B," some 250 feet long, from *Railway Age Gazette*, October 7, 1910. The elevation shows the towers as two parts of the same building—Tower A consisting of the upper two stories and Tower B of the lower two stories. The towers were separated only by the floor of the train yard's upper (long-distance) level.

38

"In the old days, when the tracks were open to the sky, it took an army of men to throw the switches by hand in the terminal yards. Later, with the coming of the control of switches from the towers, it took a smaller army to throw the long levers back and forth. That was called the manual system. Then came the automatic system, that was worked by compressed air, then the combination of air and electricity. Now it is electricity alone that does the work. Three or four men pacing to and fro in front of a long row of little handles now set the interlocking switches and the signals."
—*RAILWAY AND LOCOMOTIVE ENGINEERING*, MARCH 1913

"In this room there is something that looks like a handsomely finished oaken case. It is about seventy-five feet long, about as high as an ordinary upright piano and about as wide. Inside, but concealed from view, is a maze of electric

wires—slender cords that resemble the seeming tangle at the back of a big telephone switchboard. In front, breast high, is a double row of metal handles, each with a straight grip a hand's breadth long, one up and one down alternately."
—*NEW YORK TIMES*, FEBRUARY 2, 1913

"To each 40 levers a man is assigned who works under the instruction of a train director.... When [an incoming] train has passed down Park Ave. as far as 72d St. an electric light located on the director's desk informs him that the train has passed that point, so that the director may decide upon what track to receive the train and then call his orders to the levermen accordingly. The moment the incoming track is determined ... this information is transmitted from the signal tower by a telautograph to similar instruments located in other parts of the terminal. One of these informs the attendant at the incoming bulletin board of train movements for the convenience

of people meeting friends. Other recording instruments at various points notify the 200 station porters of the approach of all through trains."
—*ENGINEERING NEWS-RECORD*, SEPTEMBER 9, 1920

"The machine for the suburban level [Tower B] is the largest ever constructed."
—*NEW YORK TIMES*, FEBRUARY 2, 1913

38 The interlocking machine in Tower A, 1989. *Photograph by Frank English*

39 The Tower A model board, which was in use for eighty years. The lights on the board indicate signal positions, 1989. *Photograph by Frank English*

40 A tower director in Tower A, 1939.

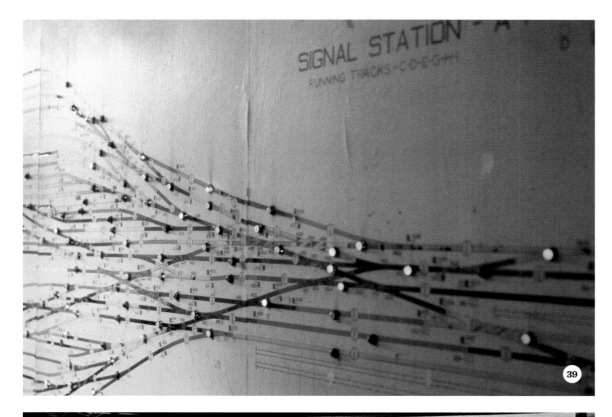

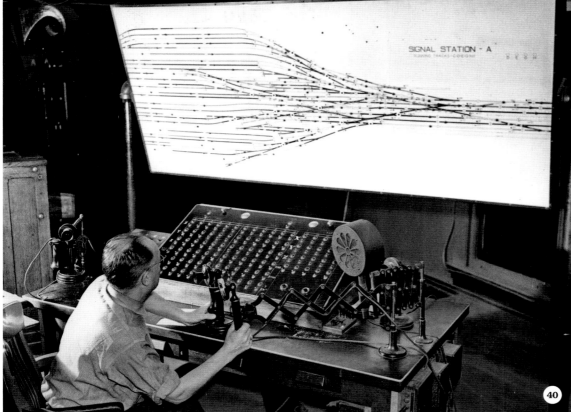

"The tower director looks over to the men standing before the long row of handles and says, '124' or '53.' Each handle has a number above it. The man who has the number called within his division of the long box pulls the corresponding handle. As he does so he feels a tiny thrill that is the indication that the 'high field' motor that controls the switch is doing the work. Then there is a gentle click, which is the second 'indication' telling of the release of the armature magnet. A little square of round glass above the handle is illuminated and shows that the switch and signal are set. Another little circle lights up on the tower director's map, another number is called, and so on until the train or the engine is at the end of its journey."
—*NEW YORK TIMES*, FEBRUARY 2, 1913

"Should the tower director call a wrong number or should one of the men misunderstand him and pull the wrong lever the electric indicators would show the error at once. Not only that, but that particular section of the interlocking system of switches and signals on the tracks outside would show it to the eyes of the engineer. Even if the engineer did not see it the train would be 'tripped' automatically and brought to a stop until the error was rectified. This signal tower below the surface of the street is the last word in electrical control of trains."
—*RAILWAY AND LOCOMOTIVE ENGINEERING*, MARCH 1913

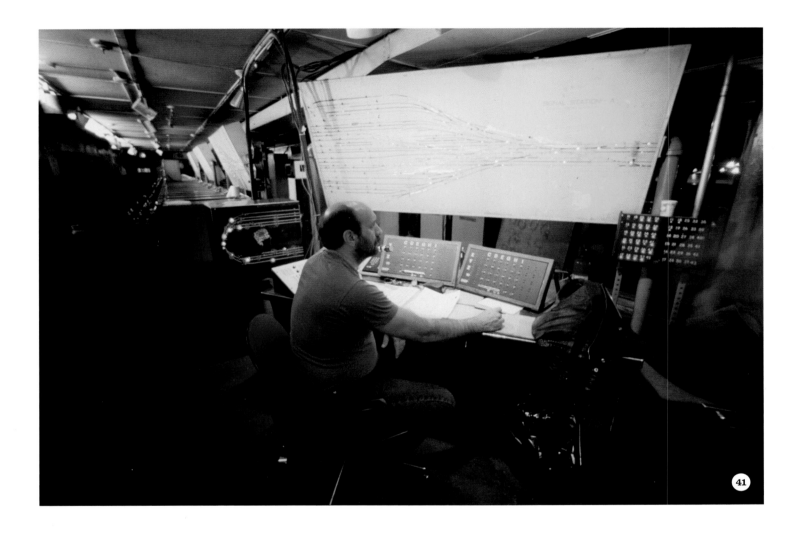

41

"Over at one side of the room ... a man sits at a desk on which a telegraph instrument chatters intermittently. On a frame of ground glass beside him is etched a map of tracks in the terminal, spreading out fanwise from the mouth of the tunnel under Park Avenue. A little circle about half the diameter of a dime marks the point where each track branches off. As soon as the train 'hits the hill'—as they call emerging from the tunnel mouth—the first bulb lights behind the first of these little circles. The tower director— the man at the telegraph key—knows that the train is coming ... and knows just what he is going to do with it, just where he is going to place it, as soon as it gets within his reach."

—*NEW YORK TIMES*, FEBRUARY 2, 1913

"The movement of the trains is indicated by little electric lights on a chart which is a facsimile of the track layout of the yards. As the trains pass over the switches the lights on the chart are extinguished and not relighted until the train has passed over the switch onto the next one.... So accurately is the movement of the trains indicated by the little electric lights on the chart ... that the exact position of every train at every moment is known, even to the point of the last car's location and that of the front of the electric motor. Nor is such a mass of important detail rendered burdensome and therefore confusing to the operators. Like the accurate vision of the eye, the brain of the terminal takes in without apparent effort the entire situation. 'At a glance' is the only word for it."

—*NEW YORK TIMES*, FEBRUARY 2, 1913

41 A tower director in Tower A, c. 1993. *Photograph by Frank English*

42 The destruction of Tower B in a fire in 1986 led to the complete replacement of the interlocking machines and five towers with a new centrally located computerized system in the Terminal's upper stories. *Photograph by Frank English*

43 The new Metro-North Operations Control Center, 2010. A computerized map replaces the former model board but, like its predecessor, replicates the tracks in the Terminal, the Park Avenue Tunnel, and part of the three commuter rail lines. Rail traffic controllers sit facing computer monitors that show exact replicas of the portion of the board they control. *Photograph by Patrick Cashin*

Grand Central Terminal: Computerized Operations Control Center

"The smokey fire that destroyed Tower B on Sunday Evening September 21, seriously wounded operations of Metro-North trains at Grand Central Terminal, threw time schedules and track assignments into disarray, disrupted the commuting plans of most of the railroad's 90,000 customers, and shocked the smoothly running rail system into an awareness of its maddening vulnerability."

—*ON TRACK* (THE MONTHLY NEWS PUBLICATION FOR METRO-NORTH EMPLOYEES), NOVEMBER 1986

"From deep in the heart of Texas—home of the Cowboys and the first computer chip—comes the soul of what will be a new era in train control at Metro-North. General Railway Signal of Dallas manufactured the majority of the computer equipment that will operate the railroad's new 'super tower.' When the facility is completed and 'cut in' to control traffic flow in Grand Central, such old soldiers as Towers A, B, C, U, NICK, and the infamous MO will be laid to rest. The changeover will see the railroad go from one of the oldest—albeit tried and true—signal control systems using levers to a state-of-the-art system relying on microprocessors using computer chips."

—*ON TRACK* (THE MONTHLY NEWS PUBLICATION FOR METRO-NORTH EMPLOYEES), FEBRUARY 1992

44

"The traffic-control room is home to roughly two dozen controllers who watch every move and hear every sound along the routes serving Grand Central, represented by colorful schematics on computer screens. Training alone takes about five years, and most controllers have three decades of experience. 'You need ice in your veins,' [assistant chief rail traffic controller] Mr. Fahey said with a grin. 'You come in here, your blood pressure goes up five points when you walk in the door.'"
—*NEW YORK TIMES*, NOVEMBER 26, 2009

"The packed train raced toward its final stop in Midtown, a thousand weary commuters aboard. Thirty seconds down the track, a train running in the opposite direction seemed to be heading straight toward it. High above Grand Central Terminal, in the station's secluded rail-traffic control office, the disquieting scene unfolded on a monitor watched by a team of focused controllers. A call was made, a track was switched, and the trains shot by each other with time to spare.... 'It's organized chaos,' said Tom Hennessy, the station's yardmaster for two decades, who dealt with several similar situations on Wednesday.

'You don't exactly know how you'll do it, but you know you'll get it done.'"
—*NEW YORK TIMES*, NOVEMBER 26, 2009

45

"The room is perhaps not solemn to the men, but it seems so to you. The air is heavy with duty. You do not speak. You would shrink back at the very touch of those great levers, nor can you be induced, hardly, to throw one, though you are told it is not in use and you are invited to throw it by way of explanation. Should one of the operators turn to address you for a moment, you instinctively ask him not to take his eyes off his work."

—*NEW YORK TIMES*, FEBRUARY 2, 1913

44 Track 25, the "nerve center" of the train shed, 2009. The office looks for anything that might go wrong throughout the train shed: with the tracks, signals, electrical systems, train crew, or passengers requiring medical attention. *Photograph by Frank English*

45 Power supervisors in the power control room, c. 2006. *Photograph by Frank English*

6
POWER

Electrification of the train service at Grand Central Terminal led to sinking the tracks and train yard beneath the city streets, out of sight. The physical plants providing heat and electric power originally stayed above ground, in a boiler house and substation just east of Park Avenue between 49th and 50th streets. The twin smokestacks of the boiler house once towered over neighboring buildings. By 1930, both boiler house and substation had disappeared—replaced by the Waldorf-Astoria hotel—with the substation relocated seven blocks south and ten stories down below the Graybar Building, in a facility carved out of the city's bedrock. Moving the equipment from the old location to the new required a massive effort, making use of the underground tracks linking 50th Street with the Terminal. A hidden reminder of the 50th Street buildings still exists directly below the Waldorf: the train yard's storage tracks, once used by train cars to collect and cart off boiler house ashes. Those tracks include the mysterious Track 61 and its "presidential siding."

"The buildings in the terminal area are erected over the tracks of the yard and consequently where ordinarily in the buildings the heating, lighting and power machinery is located, trains are running back and forth. To overcome this condition, a power and heating plant of great magnitude was erected at Fiftieth street between Lexington and Park avenues and therein is assembled the machinery for lighting and heating all the buildings in the terminal and both present and prospective."

—*BANKERS' MAGAZINE*, JANUARY 1913

1 The substation and boiler house over the train yard at 50th Street, the future site of the Waldorf-Astoria hotel, 1914. The photo shows just how far the train yard extends beneath the buildings, from Park Avenue on the left all the way to Lexington Avenue on the right. None of the buildings over the train yard have traditional foundations and basements, because they all rest on enormous steel girders. *Courtesy of Warren & Wetmore Collection, Avery Architectural & Fine Arts Library, Columbia University*

The 50th Street Substation and Boiler House

The New York Central first approached the issue of accessing electric and steam power for its new Terminal and trains by building its own power generators, substations, and boiler houses—a solution not uncommon at the time. Two power plants to the north, at Port Morris in the Bronx and at Yonkers, generated 11,000-volt, twenty-five-cycle alternating current, fed to a new substation at 50th Street just east of Park Avenue. The substation converted the alternating current to the 660-volt direct current required by the New York Central's 800-ton locomotives. The substation was located in a wing of the boiler house, a large building with two tall smokestacks. Because of the unprecedented collection of huge buildings supported on girders in the train yard, Grand Central's 50th Street substation and boiler house had to provide electricity, heat, and hot water not just for the Terminal and its trains, but also for all the buildings surrounding its site.

14836-B- Building on 49th St.
South Elevation Boiler House

5-22-2

2 New York Central's boiler house and substation on 49th Street in 1929, shortly before their demolition to make way for the Waldorf-Astoria. The view is looking north along Park Lane, a private street, no longer existing, running from 48th to 49th streets between Park and Lexington avenues. Park Lane was opened in 1923 behind the new Park Lane Hotel, which faced Park Avenue, in order to maximize light and air; it also provided parking for hotel guests.

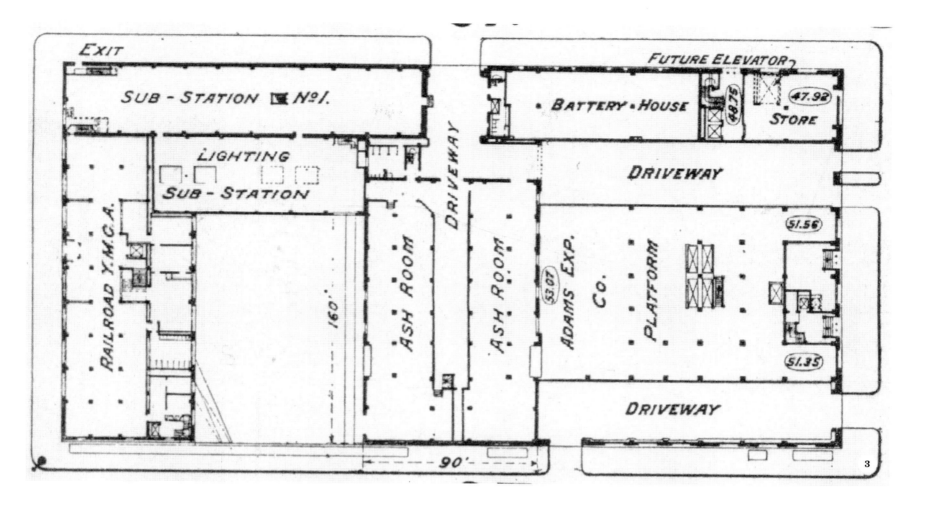

"It is one of the most striking things about the terminal city that it will be an array of buildings without any real basements—without any basements that are really at the base of the buildings. In the buildings already completed ... the 'basements' are on the fourth floor. They call these quarters 'basements' because they are dedicated to purposes usually fulfilled by basements. They have storage rooms, and they accommodate the big pipes from which radiate the myriad pipes to heat the rooms. For all the buildings of the Grand Central group will be heated from one power and heating plant, the one already erected at Fiftieth Street, between Park and Lexington Avenues. Having no basements of their own, the buildings of the group ... will have to depend on the machinery housed at Fiftieth Street."

—*NEW YORK TIMES*, FEBRUARY 2, 1913

"The service plant furnishes electricity for lighting, the operation of elevator and other motors, heat for all buildings within the terminal, and steam for heating of cars in the station. Fire and service pumps, freight-elevator pumps, compressors and miscellaneous pumps and boiler-plant auxiliaries are also installed. The service station is primarily a heating plant. Steam required for heating cars within the terminal is drawn from the boilers through reducing valves.... The heating of all the various buildings within the terminal area is by hot water, heated by the exhaust steam of the various units in the power plant.... The water is heated in three large 'even-flow' exhaust-steam heaters, and is circulated by suitable motor-driven centrifugal pumps.... Coal is delivered either by cars on the track level, or by trucks on the street level."

—*POWER*, MAY 20, 1913

3 Plan of the boiler house and substation, 1912; 49th Street is at the bottom, 50th Street at the top.

14835-B- Building on 50th St G.C.T. North Elevation Boiler House + Service plant. 5-22-29

"The extent of the power and heating plant facilities serving the terminal layout is indicated by the fact that on the coldest days the coal consumption reaches 500 tons, and the average boiler load per day during a cold month is about 5,000,000 lbs. of steam.... Both steam and hot water heating systems are used and the hot water mains alone have a total length of over four miles.... A complete refrigeration plant is also included in the power units.... From the 50th St. plant hot water for heating purposes is driven a mile in its circuit to most of the buildings in the group including the main station building the incoming station, the terminal offices, the Post Office, general office building, the Vanderbilt Concourse Offices, Grand Central Palace, the Yale Club, the Biltmore Hotel, the Express Building and the Y.M.C.A., the last being in the same block as the 50th St. power plant. Three stages of pressure are necessary to provide for the great height to which hot water is raised in connection with heating the Biltmore Hotel."
—*ENGINEERING NEWS-RECORD*, SEPTEMBER 9, 1920

"The [water] mains are divided into three groups, carrying different pressures to conform to the height of the building. A building seven stories high is connected to the low pressure system; buildings above this height up to seventeen stories use the intermediate pressure system for the section above the part taken by the low-pressure system, while stories beyond seventeen, up to and including twenty-seven stories, are supplied by the high-pressure system. This hot-water heating system, with its provision for extension, is the largest of its kind existing, and will be ample to supply a town having between 6000 and 7000 standard country homes.... The water circulated through these systems is not wasted, but is reheated and pumped continuously throughout the system, all of the exhaust steam available from the steam turbines and auxiliaries at the service plant being used for heating, supplemented by live steam when the heating loads exceed the amount of exhaust steam available."
—*RAILWAY REVIEW*, AUGUST 1915

"From the roof of that plant two huge smokestacks rise to a towering height. These smokestacks are interesting, for they are the only ones in the whole thirty blocks. And when the thirty blocks have all been 'improved' they will remain the solitary smokestacks of that part of New York. Even they are equipped with the last word in smoke consumers, so that, even when it is a completed and thriving area, the terminal city will be smokeless. That is one element in the promised beauty."
—*NEW YORK TIMES*, FEBRUARY 2, 1913

S- C-23 - 12 -18 -23
G.C. Termina 1 - South From - 51- St

5

"[The use of] smokeless stacks ... means economical service, as well as saving of space and avoidance of smoke and dirt in all present and future buildings, none of which will require a boiler room or a chimney. There will also be less danger of fire."

—*NEW-YORK TRIBUNE*, DECEMBER 15, 1912

"The fire signal system that has been installed is comparable to that of a small modern city."

—*RAILWAY REVIEW*, FEBRUARY 5, 1921

4 Boiler house and service plant on the south side of 50th Street, looking toward Lexington Avenue, 1929.

5 Smokeless towers of the 50th Street boiler house, 1926. The towers were equipped with "smoke consumers" that eliminated most smoke. To the right, Park Avenue extends south to the original 45th Street facade of Grand Central Terminal.

"The construction of this building was done in a rush, as the old plant had been put out of service in the summer of 1910....two of the boilers in the new building [were functioning] on October 15, 1910, although there were no sides to the building at that time ... Adjoining this building there is the rotary lighting substation, which is 109 ft. long, 40 ft. wide and 73 ft. high above the track level, and the building contains the rotary converters, transformers, switchboards, and other apparatus to supply electricity throughout the terminal, for all purposes except traction. At present there are installed two rotary converters of 1500 k.w. capacity. There is a balancer set of 130 k.w. capacity, and space for two additional converters."

—*RAILWAY REVIEW*, AUGUST 1915

"The ashes ... can be discharged through chutes to cars underneath the building."

—*RAILWAY REVIEW*, AUGUST 1915

"Among the wholesale business secured by The New York Edison Company is the group of 30 large buildings in the Grand Central Terminal area, formerly supplied by The New York Central and Hudson River Railroad Company, with installations aggregating about 30,000 kilowatts, and an annual consumption exceeding 50,000,000 kilowatt hours."

—*CONSOLIDATED GAS COMPANY OF NEW YORK AND ITS AFFILIATED GAS AND ELECTRIC COMPANIES, ANNUAL REPORT*, 1927

6 50th Street substation under construction, 1906. *Courtesy of the Grand Central Collection, Archives Center, National Museum of American History, Smithsonian Institution*

Moving the Substation to Its New Home

"The magnitude of this moving job becomes apparent when one considers that the engineers were compelled to dismantle the plant, move much of it the distance of seven blocks, and add new apparatus, without interfering with the operation of the terminal or of the trains entering it, without hampering street traffic, which is quite heavy, and finish the job on a scheduled date which necessitated the work being placed on an emergency basis."
—*SCIENTIFIC AMERICAN*, JUNE 1930

By 1927, New York Central had contracted out much of its electricity production to the New York Edison Company (predecessor to Con Edison), buying power in bulk from the utility, but continuing to distribute that power to the Terminal and the surrounding buildings of Terminal City. The original boiler house and substation at 50th Street continued functioning until 1930, by which time the rise in property values along Park Avenue all but required the removal of the power station to make way for the skyscraping Waldorf-Astoria. The New York Central gave up its steam operation, contracting out instead to the New York Steam Corporation, while moving the electric substation en masse to a new underground location carved out of solid rock, 100 feet below the Graybar Building. Part of this underground area had been excavated earlier to house several boilers; with the boilers removed and additional space excavated, this location became the world's largest power substation.

"Work in preparing the block bounded by Park and Lexington Avenues, Forty-ninth and Fiftieth Streets, for the new Waldorf Hotel will begin tomorrow with the demolition of the New York Central's great electric and steam plants in that block which supply power, light, steam heat and hot water for the group of apartment houses, hotels and office buildings between Fiftieth Street and the Grand Central Terminal, as well as for railroad purposes. The plant, which contains the electrical converters through which passes the current providing power and light for trains and buildings, will be torn down and its electric and mechanical facilities shifted a quarter mile south to the Grand Central Terminal."
—*NEW YORK TIMES*, MARCH 31, 1929

"It was necessary to transfer, among other material, an 8,000 ampere electric storage battery consisting of 150 tanks weighing 5,000 pounds each. In every tank were lead plates submerged in sulphuric acid. As it is against the law to transport such open tanks of acid through the city streets, the New York Central made use of tunnels that run through the terminal.... "
—*SCIENTIFIC AMERICAN*, JUNE 1930

7   Silhouette of the proposed Waldorf-Astoria hotel, superimposed over the buildings then on the site, including the boiler house and substation. The view is looking to the northeast, across the train yard tracks and Park Avenue, 1917. The tracks beneath the site had been covered over by 1930 when the substation was relocated to 43rd Street, but were still available to transport machinery between the old and new substations. Machinery was lowered through hatches into freight cars below the building, and then moved by rail to the new substation without incident. Contemporary accounts called the task "unprecedented."

The New Substation: 100 Feet Below the Terminal

"In the heart of Manhattan, 100 feet down in the solid rock below Forty-third Street and Lexington Avenue, the world's largest electric substation and hot-water heating plant is being rapidly completed for the New York Central Railroad Company.... The old plant's equipment ... is now being torn down and shifted to the new site.... All the work of erection and transfer has had to be done at record speed, without disturbing the hundreds of train movements daily or so much as holding up an elevator or in any way inconveniencing passengers or tenants of the Terminal Building. The new substation will be four stories deep, covering a site 250 feet long by 50 feet wide under Forty-third Street. It will have a preliminary capacity of 25,000 kilowatts, with room for expansion up to 32,600."
—*NEW YORK TIMES*, DECEMBER 1, 1929

"The present site of the substation—an excavation about 90 feet deep and 225 feet long by 60 feet wide—had previously been made in the solid rock under 43rd Street, to accommodate a boiler plant. Two boilers were installed, with room for four more. This plant consisted of four floors: a basement, a boiler room, a meter room, and the coal bunkers. The stack extended to the top of the Commodore Hotel and was concealed in that structure. Another vast cellar was also dug out under the southern end of the Graybar Building.... Calculations then established the fact that it would be possible to utilize the great stone vault, intended for the boiler plant, as the new site of the substation."
—*SCIENTIFIC AMERICAN*, JUNE 1930

"Years ago the engineers of the New York Central Lines foresaw the possibility that they would some day have to transfer the heating plant to Forty-third Street, and they kept free a large excavation in that section. Plans for this new structure were laid out even before the Graybar Building was constructed, and when the time came for demolishing the old power house at Fiftieth Street everything was in readiness. ... The new plant is cradled in the bedrock of the island. Great steel beams and pillars support the weight above. Thousands of feet of pipe and wire wind in and out. Heavy armatures, when they are being lowered by cranes into the depths, vaguely resemble divers going to explore the sea bottom."
—*NEW YORK TIMES*, DECEMBER 1, 1929

8   Metro-North substation 1T ejector room. The twin 100-gallon, compressed-air ejectors pump water out of the basement.

9   Metro-North substation 1T-L staircase. The new home of the power station was carved out of solid rock 100 feet below ground—the equivalent of a ten-story building in depth.

10   Grand Central Terminal substation 1T-L. The rotary converters functioned until July 1989, when they were decommissioned and replaced with more modern solid state equipment. *Photographs by Gerald Weinstein, 1984*

8

9

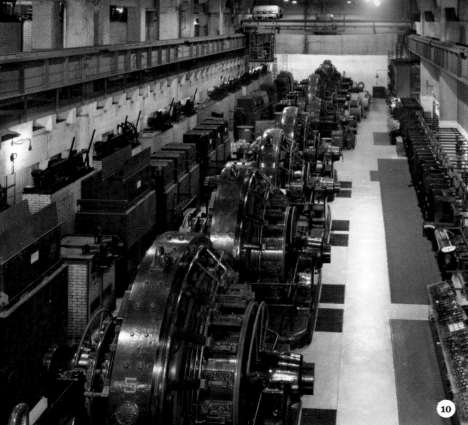

10

"The new plant contains only the most up-to-date equipment. Five large General Electric rotary transformers will convert traction power for trains, totaling 17,000 kilowatts. Five other converters will provide 8,000 kilowatts of electric current for lighting and for elevators. One electric and two traction rotaries are already in operation and the others will be put in service as soon as installed. Three of these rotaries, each with a capacity of 4,000 kilowatts, are brand new and represent the latest in size and force. The others are being brought from the former plant at Fiftieth Street.... Air for cooling the apparatus will be drawn down into the subterranean depths through the ash hoist once used in conjunction with the former boiler plant."

—*NEW YORK TIMES*, DECEMBER 1, 1929

"The total weight of this apparatus and other major electrical machinery installed was 850 tons. All of this had to be lowered piece by piece a vertical distance of fifty feet from the unloading platform to the substation main floor.... Every cubic foot from the basement to the street level was utilized for electrical purposes, and this apparatus was in service at all times in the great work of operating all the trains in the terminal area and lighting the great group of buildings crowning it."

—*NEW YORK CENTRAL LINES MAGAZINE*, MARCH 1930

"Light, heat, and power is distributed by this plant to more than 60,000 persons occupying floor space exceeding 256 acres. This plant provides the electricity which illuminates 100,000 or more electric lights, moves more than 650 trains daily, operates 325 elevators in 28 buildings, and supplies these buildings—among the largest in the world—with the hot water which heats some, the steam that heats others, and hot water for general purposes. It also distributes steam to warm innumerable railroad cars, and it compresses air, not only for railroad purposes, but to open and close hundreds of elevator doors in the buildings, to assist in cleaning, and for other uses."

—*SCIENTIFIC AMERICAN*, JUNE 1930

11 Substation rotary converter control board, 1992. *Photograph by Frank English*

12 A rotary converter in the Metro-North substation 1T-L, 1984. *Photograph by Gerald Weinstein*

"It was necessary to design and install an entirely new set of switchboards for the lighting and traction substations and an extension of the switchboard of lighting substation 1-B; to provide a large system of air filters to cleanse the air entering the substations, battery room and air compressors. Part of the ventilation system involved the provision of an air intake ten feet by ten feet square cut through solid rock, so that half the air entering the substation should come from the suburban loop track area, where additional terminal ventilation was necessary."

—*NEW YORK CENTRAL LINES MAGAZINE*, MARCH 1930

13 DC lighting breaker board in the interior of the Metro-North substation 1L that controlled lighting throughout the Grand Central complex.

14 Rear view of breaker panel inside Metro-North Substation 1T-L, 1984. *Photographs by Gerald Weinstein*

"The facilities removed have been placed so deeply underground that they will never be a nuisance or interfere with the full development of the terminal. They operate in their new surroundings as efficiently and as reliably as in their former locations.... The result of the operation is to remove from the Fiftieth Street block a collection of buildings out of harmony with the splendor of Grand Central Terminal and to permit the erection on their site of a monumental building of surpassing beauty."

—*NEW YORK CENTRAL LINES MAGAZINE*, MARCH 1930

15 Emergency water-supply pipes in the service plant at the Terminal, c. 2006. *Photograph by Frank English*

16 One of the passageways within Grand Central Terminal with several large steam pipes and valves, 1985. Because of the oppressive heat, Terminal staff know these passageways as "Burma Road." *Photograph by Frank English*

Track 61:
The Waldorf-Astoria and the "Presidential Siding"

"The new Waldorf-Astoria Hotel … will have a private railway siding underneath the building, it was learned yesterday. Guests with private rail cars may have them routed directly to the hotel … and may leave their cars at a special elevator which will take them directly to their suites or to the lobby. The arrangement is made possible because of the fact that the New York Central tracks pass directly beneath the block."
—*NEW YORK TIMES*, SEPTEMBER 8, 1929

New York City underground lore has long included the story of Franklin D. Roosevelt's "presidential siding"—a train spur beneath the Waldorf-Astoria. Much of the story remains mysterious, but the siding exists, and FDR did use it on at least one occasion, as did several other public figures. The spur in question predates the hotel. The Waldorf replaced several Terminal City buildings—the Adams Express Company, a YMCA for railroad employees, and the 50th Street boiler house and substation—all located above the storage tracks at the north end of the New York Central's train yard. When the new hotel opened, the management announced that a siding alongside one of the tracks would be available to accept delivery of hotel supplies—and also to accommodate private rail cars, the ultimate convenience for its wealthiest patrons. An elevator connects the siding with an entrance on the 49th Street side of the hotel, adjacent to the Waldorf's underground car garage.

Those known to have used the siding include two generals (John J. Pershing in 1938 and Douglas MacArthur in 1951); one president (FDR, while campaigning for reelection in October 1944); and one presidential contender (Illinois governor Adlai Stevenson, around the time he first ran unsuccessfully against Dwight D. Eisenhower). The siding also attracted partygoers, including those attending a press event in 1948, a benefit dinner in 1955, and an Andy Warhol happening in 1965. More prosaically, the siding provided a location for showing off new locomotives in 1946 and 1956—at the 1946 event, the siding was opened for two days to the general public, perhaps the only time on record. In 1978, the *Christian Science Monitor* reported that the Waldorf was "seriously thinking of reopening its private railroad siding to accommodate VIPs arriving via Amtrak," but that apparently never happened.

17 The elevator at Track 61. *Courtesy of the Waldorf-Astoria*

18 The elevator at street level. *Photograph by Sam Horine*

"The new Waldorf-Astoria is really going to have it on the other hotels in various and sundry ways, unless its publicity man is like unto the theatrical press agent and doesn't really mean what he says. The latest is that the New York Central is going to run a private railroad siding under the new inn. Then you say to the Rock Island division superintendent, 'Route this car to the Waldorf-Astoria' and when you wake up in the morning there you are under the hotel and a special elevator carries you and your baggage right upstairs to your room!"
—*ARCHITECT*, VOLUME 13, 1929

"The speech [of Saturday night, October 21, 1944] over with, a Secret Service agent rescued Grace Tully and me from the throng of diners and we went down in the hotel elevator with the President and Mrs. Roosevelt to the spur track which was put in at the construction of the new Waldorf-Astoria for the accommodation of the private cars of 'economic royalists'—never, however, used but twice: once by General Pershing when he was ill, and now, of all persons, by the archfoe of the privileged group for whose delectation this extravagant convenience was devised. Another irony of fate."
—*OFF THE RECORD WITH F.D.R., 1942–1945* (THE PRIVATE DIARY OF ROOSEVELT'S AIDE WILLIAM D. HASSETT)

"Travel came to a practical standstill yesterday in Grand Central Station.... William Filene's Sons Company store in Boston, in cooperation with the New Haven Railroad, was staging a genuine Cape Cod beach party and fashion show.... Executives of the New Haven Railroad and Filene's were hosts to representatives of the New York, Boston, and Cape Cod press ... at an appropriate 'shore' luncheon aboard 'The Whaler,' crack Colonial diner of the New Haven.... There was some mystery about finding the rendezvous of 'The Whaler,' which was run on the presidential siding under the Waldorf-Astoria and entered by an inconspicuous elevator from 49th Street. More excitement ensued when Mr. Boyer, instead of following the original plan and taking the guests by taxi back to the station after luncheon, located an extra engine to attach to the special cars and with much cheering took us right into the station as if we'd just arrived from Boston on the Yankee Clipper."
—*CHRISTIAN SCIENCE MONITOR*, JUNE 11, 1948

"General MacArthur and his party returned to New York at 9:50 o'clock last night on the special train. The General's private car and the observation car, from which MacArthur's five-star flag was flying, were run off onto the "presidential siding" beneath the Waldorf-Astoria Hotel. Employes [sic] of the hotel had rolled out a red carpet across the platform to an elevator. General MacArthur, in uniform, and Mrs. MacArthur, in a dark blue ensemble, posed for press photographers with Frederic C. Dumaine Jr., president of the New Haven Railroad, and Mrs. Dumaine, who had accompanied them. The party then entered the elevator and was taken to the MacArthur suite."
—*NEW YORK TIMES*, JULY 27, 1951

AMERICA "TO OUR PRESIDENT"

From [Howard] Chandler Christy

Souvenir Program

The BIRTHDAY BALL *for the* PRESIDENT

Waldorf-Astoria Hotel, January 30, 1934

DING

20

19 Program for the first FDR Birthday Ball Dinner held at the Waldorf Astoria Hotel. *Courtesy of the FDR Library*

20 General Pershing on arriving at the Waldorf-Astoria. *Reprinted courtesy of the* New York Times, *April 21, 1938*

"With a brave show of his old 'Black Jack' manner, General John J. Pershing came to New York yesterday for his son's wedding…. It was obvious that the commander of the A.E.F. had not fully recovered from the heart disease with which he had been gravely ill…. Elaborate precautions were taken to save the general from any undue exertion…. From Grand Central Station his special railroad car was shunted to a ramp under the Hotel Waldorf-Astoria that had never been used before. Inspector Charles L. Neidig was on hand with more than 100 patrolmen and detectives. General Pershing remained in his car while Dr. Roland Davison, his physician, took in the situation…. Dr. Davison told photographers and reporters, 'It has been a hard trip for the general, and I can only permit him to stand a minute or two.' Then at 8:25 A.M. the general emerged, surrounded by detectives. When he saw the photographers General Pershing smilingly said, 'Hello, boys,' and saluted."

—*NEW YORK TIMES*, APRIL 21, 1938

"Most readers of The Morning Herald know, of course, that there is a special spur track to the basement of the Waldorf—the Presidential siding, as it is called. Thus, whenever necessary, a train can be operated to New York and run right into the hotel property, whence its passengers can be conveyed without any taxi or other transfer trouble immediately to their rooms by fast elevators. It was to this special siding that the Atchison, Topeka & Santa Fe Railroad dispatched its latest acquisition—a giant-sized, streamlined, silver and red engine of 6,000 horse-power—the 75,000th locomotive, by the way, built by the American Locomotive Company. The monster was on display for several days, and was viewed by many thousands of people, all of whom, doubtless, were duly impressed."

—*MORNING HERALD [GLOVERSVILLE AND JOHNSTOWN, N.Y.],* OCTOBER 5, 1946

"The 139 food editors attending the [eleventh annual Food Editors Conference] have ... taken a special New Haven Railroad train from the famous presidential siding at the Waldorf-Astoria Hotel to Stamford, Conn., to see the Fleischmann Laboratories of Standard Brands, Inc. The train left at an early hour from the world's most exclusive railroad siding.... The excitement of such royal treatment almost overshadowed the trip through the laboratories."

—*LONG ISLAND STAR-JOURNAL,* OCTOBER 7, 1954

"The private railroad siding of the Waldorf-Astoria Hotel, rarely used except for Presidential visits, will receive tonight a special train bringing Westchester guests to the New Year's Eve Donor Dinner Cotillion of the Westchester Chapter of the Muscular Dystrophy Associations of America."

—*NEW YORK TIMES,* DECEMBER 31, 1955

A Locomotive at the Waldorf

TRANSPORTATION history is being made today at the Waldorf-Astoria. On the hotel's Private Siding a 6000-horsepower diesel-electric locomotive of significant new design will make its debut to the railroad and business world.

This is the first of a new line of passenger locomotives which shortly will go into service on the crack streamline trains of the Santa Fe Railroad.

These super-locomotives offer the American railroads a new solution to their key problem as they move into a period of vigorous, resourceful competition—the problem of providing the finest transportation for the lowest possible cost.

This is the mightiest of an entirely new line of mass-produced diesel-electric passenger and freight locomotives and switchers built by two great engineering firms, American Locomotive and the General Electric Company. From American Locomotive come the 16 cylinder V-type diesel engines which pack more power into less weight than any other locomotives on the rails. From General Electric come the war-born superchargers and new electrical equipment.

This is the 75,000th locomotive produced in more than a century by American Locomotive, builder of more locomotives than any other manufacturer in the world.

This is a proud day on the Private Siding of the Waldorf—proud for the builders of a new champion—proud for the Santa Fe Railroad which has a new technological triumph to offer its passengers between Chicago and the West.

American Locomotive Company

THE MARK OF MODERN ENGINEERING

TO BE EXHIBITED AT DEARBORN STREET STATION ANNEX OCTOBER 1ST AND 2ND

21

"An underground party was given Wednesday night in honor of Andy Warhol, artist, moviemaker and party-goer extraordinary. The scene was the private railroad siding underneath the Waldorf-Astoria Hotel on Park Ave. Host of the party was Dick Ekstract, editor and publisher of Tape Recording magazine. It was one of those marvelous blends of good fellowship and good business. The high fidelity trade show was in town. Andy Warhol had made some 'underground' tapes for one of the exhibitors at the show and Tape Magazine [*sic*] happened to have a cover story on Andy Warhol and his underground tapes. The party itself was taped, and then played back to the guests. Among the happenings by the railroad yard siding, sort of an Elizabethan duel with swords."

—*HERALD TRIBUNE*, 1965

21 American Locomotive Company advertisement, which appeared in newspapers throughout the country, 1946.

22 Illinois governor Adlai Stevenson, who lost the presidential election of 1952 to General Dwight D. Eisenhower, in the Waldorf-Astoria elevator, arriving at Track 61, c. 1952. *Courtesy of the Waldorf-Astoria*

7 MARKETS, MAIL AND MOVIE STARS

Though Grand Central became the heart of Terminal City, it also functioned—and still does—as a city unto itself. Today's Grand Central has been reimagined as a destination for New Yorkers, but in fact, the Terminal has always attracted people for reasons other than transportation.

Do out-of-towners come to New York for its art schools and galleries? Grand Central once hosted one of the largest of each, not to mention a pair of enormous artists' studios hidden among the rafters. Is New York a national media center? CBS built the country's largest television studio in the Terminal.

The tiny Grand Central Theater became famous for its newsreels. The post office coordinated the nation's mail with the Terminal's vast train traffic. New Yorkers have been devouring bivalves at the Oyster Bar for a full century, and now have the option of shopping for luxury comestibles at the new Grand Central Market. The galleries, art school, and CBS studios are long gone, while the Oyster Bar and the post office survive. John W. Campbell's fantasy hideaway in an obscure corner of the Terminal disappeared for a while, but has returned as the Campbell Apartment, a lounge open to the public. And throughout the century, the Terminal has continued to bring its special glamour and drama to the world by serving as the backdrop to American movies for more than eighty years.

"The two [concourse levels] ... are surrounded on three sides by interconnected passages along which run rows of stores: food, liquor, flower, apparel, book-, and barbershops; restaurants; newspaper and magazine stands; telegraph and theater ticket agencies; lunch and milk bars. A newsreel theater, an art gallery, Travelers' Aid service, and recreational exhibits are available in the building. All these facilities, reached by underground corridors from adjacent hotels and office buildings, make Grand Central also a neighborhood shopping center."
—*WPA GUIDE TO NEW YORK CITY*, 1939

1 Grand Central Theatre. *Courtesy of the Harry Ransom Center, the Univeristy of Texas at Austin*

Grand Central Art Galleries: "Buy a Masterpiece Between Trains"

2

"The location of the galleries in a railway station is psychologically correct; there is nothing like travel to stimulate the gland of expenditure."
—*NEW YORK TIMES*, MARCH 21, 1923

In 1922, Walter L. Clark—a mechanical engineer and businessman turned artist, and a personal friend of American painter John Singer Sargent—decided to bring his business experience to the realm of his new artistic passion. He arranged to convert the Terminal's sixth-story space, facing 42nd Street, into an enormous nonprofit cooperative art gallery, occupying large skylit exhibition rooms designed by the architectural firm of Delano & Aldrich. In an unusual arrangement, a number of wealthy supporters invested a set amount of money each year, in return for which they entered an annual lottery drawing for works donated by the artists. The Grand Central Art Galleries' stated goal was to help the artists make a living by selling their work in a more businesslike way, and allowing them to keep all the proceeds, minus only a small commission to cover the expense of running the cooperative. Grand Central offered an ideal location not only because the New York Central offered the space at a modest rent, but also because the Galleries would attract the attention of summer visitors flocking to New York City through the Terminal, especially with advertising by New York Central.

Sargent died in 1925, but not before the Galleries

had mounted a huge show of his portraits. A trove of his drawings, discovered posthumously in London by Clark, became another exhibit in 1926. Occasionally, the Galleries hosted special exhibitions, notably in 1924, when the English-Speaking Union (of which Winston Churchill was chairman) loaned the Galleries paintings from the 1923 British Empire Exposition, including works by Hogarth, Reynolds, Romney, Lawrence, and Gainsborough, as well as contemporary British artists. President Calvin Coolidge sent a letter to Clark on that occasion, welcoming "all endeavors to bring about among English-speaking peoples the interchange of ideas."

In later years, the Galleries developed a reputation as "conservative" in taste, but in 1947 devoted a show to the abstract work of Stuart Davis. By 1958, when the cooperative moved across the street to the Biltmore Hotel, it represented some three hundred American artists. The Galleries had also branched out in many directions, including sponsorship of the United States Pavilion—also designed by Delano & Aldrich—at the Venice Biennale.

"The retrospective exhibition of paintings by John Singer Sargent at the Grand Central Art Galleries is proving the 'grande semaine' of the New York art season. ... All the old bogies about Mr. Sargent being only a painter of fair women ... fly out of the skylights of the Grand Central Galleries in the presence of [these portraits].... It is certain that the results of the Sargent Exhibition of 1924 will be far-reaching and of great consequence."
—*CHRISTIAN SCIENCE MONITOR*, MARCH 3, 1924

2 The Retrospective Exhibition of Important Works of John Singer Sargent, held at the Grand Central Art Galleries in 1924. *Photograph by Peter A. Juley & Son, Courtesy of the Photograph Archives, Smithsonian American Art Museum*

3 Helen Holt Hawley, flanked by Walter Clark (left) and Bruce Crane (right), draws names out of a steel jar at the annual "founders' exhibition drawing" at the Grand Central Art Galleries in 1933. *Grand Central Art Galleries Incorporated*

"Each year the lay members of the galleries make money contributions and receive in exchange the right to participate in the drawing for paintings and sculpture contributed by the artist members…. The drawing was held at 4 o'clock."

—*NEW YORK TIMES*, NOVEMBER 24, 1933

"When the Grand Central Art Galleries open on March 21 there will be inaugurated in this country a cooperative art gallery such as was never before planned for the sale of works of American art…. Walter L. Clark … realized that many artists' cooperative sales galleries or societies had been wrecked on the shoals of 'art politics' and tempermental [*sic*] differences between members who were not, primarily, business men. Therefore he worked out the idea of having the organization, as a machine for selling art works, conducted solely by the practical business men…. The artist members act only as a committee to pass on applications for membership which guarantees the quality of the works shown."

—*ART NEWS, AN INTERNATIONAL NEWSPAPER OF ART*, MARCH 17, 1923

"The real estate agent given the task of renting the number of acres required by the Clark scheme was in despair. He said it couldn't be done outside of Madison Square Garden or the Grand Central Station. 'That would be fine,' said Clark. 'What!' exclaimed the bewildered agent. 'Grand Central Station,' beamed Clark."

—*NEW YORKER*, AUGUST 1, 1925

"More than $100,000 is being spent by the New York Central Railroad and the Painters and Sculptors' Gallery Association in clearing out the sixth floor or attic of the Grand Central Terminal, and refitting it as the largest sales gallery of art in the world. The top of the building was filled with sacks of cement, cases of obsolete stationery, lumber and other material and had been in disuse since the building was erected. It will be occupied by twenty galleries when the remodeling and redecoration is completed."

—*NEW YORK TIMES*, MARCH 11, 1923

"The busy man—or busier woman—may now buy a masterpiece between trains. If the business world has no time to go to art galleries, then art galleries must go to the business world. At all events, the pioneer in this democratic venture has just swung out a shingle in the Grand Central Station…. Paintings by our best-known artists hang but a few steps from the electric locomotives that start our cross-country fliers on their way. The man from San Francisco or San Antonio may step from gallery to parlor car or vice versa without losing more than a fraction of his valuable time."

—*NEW YORK TIMES*, MARCH 18, 1923

"Most of the galleries receive direct sunlight, but this is mixed with artificial light, which is said to be the most perfect imitation of north light yet applied to a large gallery. The yellow rays are suppressed in the electric lighting, and the light rays filter through a large area of glass overhead, so that glare is avoided and diffused light obtained. Because of the perfect soft white light produced, the Illuminating Engineers' Association will study the lighting system and hold a meeting at the galleries on April 3."

—*NEW YORK TIMES*, MARCH 11, 1923

Grand Central School of Art: "One of the most completely equipped institutions of its kind in the country"

"More than a score of workmen were engaged yesterday in taking the roof off the east wing of the Grand Central Terminal in preparation for replacing it with glass skylights for the new Grand Central School of Art. The school ... will occupy 7,000 square feet of floor space, and [will be] one of the most completely equipped institutions of its kind in the country."

—*NEW YORK TIMES*, AUGUST 21, 1924

As part of its mission, the Galleries organized an art school in the Terminal—the Grand Central School of Art under the direction of Edmund Greacen—which opened October 1, 1924, next door to the Galleries. Its hundreds of students ranged from Charles Addams, whose *New Yorker* cartoons inspired *The Addams Family* TV series, to famed painter Arshile Gorky, who joined the faculty in 1926.

Another faculty member, Ezra Winter—one of the great muralists of the day, and best known in New York City for his 60 by 40–foot Fountain of Youth mural on the grand staircase at Radio City Music Hall—rented a space even higher than the Galleries and School for his studio, so high up that the Terminal's electrician had to pass through it to reach the space above the Concourse ceiling in order to service the "stars." Ac-

cording to several accounts, the space in question had been left deliberately unfinished, in case a tower addition should ever be added to the building. During the First World War, camouflage designers had worked there, making ship models on which to experiment with various shades of paint. At war's end, Winter, who'd spent time with the camouflage designers, arranged to rent the space and made it his studio. He stayed for many years—as did Augustus Vincent Tack, an artist in a neighboring studio. Winter's famous studio parties attracted well-known artists and society figures, who in turn attracted press coverage.

4 Arshile Gorky, 1936. *Photograph by Von Urban, Courtesy of the Federal Art Project, Smithsonian Institution, Archives of American Art, Photographic Division Collection*

5 Ezra Winter at work, c. 1930s. *Photograph by Peter A. Juley & Son, Courtesy of the Photograph Archives, Smithsonian American Art Museum*

"Ezra Winter has perhaps the only board walk in New York, and it's on, of all places, the top floor of Grand Central Terminal. Winter's studio, where he paints murals, is up there, too, six stories above the acres of concourse across which thousands of pigmy-like travelers stream to and from their trains. The visitor takes an elevator up to the Grand Central art gallery ... and then climbs a flight of stairs to a vast attic, cluttered with enormous pipes and gigantic machinery. The board walk leads him to the studio, which during the war was a camouflage laboratory. That is how Winter happened to move in. He was one of the artists who worked there on designs for making ships invisible. After the Armistice, when he took up mural painting, he found his studio in Macdougall alley too small for the large canvases. So now he lives and works atop one of the country's largest train terminals. With his pals, George Chamberlain, the novelist; Will Beebe, the naturalist, and William Chadbourne, lawyer and banker, Winter gives studio parties attended by notables of art, music and the drama. The red-caps in the concourse know where to send anybody they see downstairs in masquerade costume."

—*NIAGARA FALLS GAZETTE*, JUNE 27, 1929

"The incident brings to mind the remarkable exploit of Mr. Ezra Winter, the painter, whose studio is in the building that grows out of the labyrinthine roots of the Grand Central Terminal. Called into the corridor outside his rooms by a Western Union messenger one afternoon, he found himself locked out. What was worse, he was wearing only his BVDs. There was but one way to gain admittance, by a circuitous route that led, of all places for a gentleman in his linen, down into the vasty halls of the Grand Central Station itself. With as debonair a gesture as a man in his BVD's in the Grand Central can make, Mr. Winter slipped like a wraith past incredulous travellers, terrorized Red caps, and a policeman who, before he could cry 'Halt!' saw the apparition break into a run and disappear forever, at least insofar as he was concerned."

—*NEW YORKER*, JANUARY 21, 1928

CBS Studios: "The largest television studio plant in the country"

In 1937, William S. Paley of CBS installed a television transmitter on top of the Chrysler Building, just across Lexington Avenue from the Terminal—which at the time must have made the Terminal the logical place to build what CBS described as an experimental television studio. In the early years, CBS transmitted fifteen hours a week to the fewer than ten thousand television sets in and around New York—most of those being in bars. Following World War II, with the explosion of television viewing, CBS added two 700,000-cubic-foot studios at Grand Central. The network kept its studios at the Terminal through the mid-1960s, and set up a feed to a gigantic monitor in the Main Concourse, where New Yorkers could gather to watch major news events.

From its Grand Central studios, the network broadcast such long-running favorites as the quiz show *What's My Line?* and the soap operas *As the World Turns* and *Guiding Light*, as well as *Playhouse 90*, *The Goldbergs*, and coverage of the 1960 Olympics. *Douglas Edwards with the News* began what became the august tradition of the *CBS Evening News*. At various times, *The Morning Show* featured talk show host Jack Paar, actor Dick Van Dyke, and anchorman Walter Cronkite—celebrities who, along with Douglas Edwards, mingled with the Terminal's commuters every day.

"The central studio ... will contain dressing rooms, rehearsal rooms, carpentry shop, and a laboratory. Provision also has been made for the cutting, editing, and scanning of motion picture films. The project is designed to promote the first full-scale working model in this country of a complete television unit operating under typical conditions of actual daily production. The mode of operation ... is to make as many experiments as possible in order to make as many errors as possible in advance as a means of establishing television on the same standard of entertainment value as other mature arts."
—*CHICAGO DAILY TRIBUNE*, AUGUST 24, 1937

"The two studios from which the shows—drama, variety, quiz, audience participation and what not—will emanate, will be set up in much the way Hollywood sound stages are. A number of sets can be spread around the big studios, and, as one scene shifts to another, the cameras can follow with no time out for scene changes. Sponsors will now be invited to watch the whole show—of which the producers' antics are a major part— from a row of seats in the control room itself."
—*WASHINGTON POST*, FEBRUARY 22, 1948

"Tomorrow morning ... C.B.S. television will put forth 'The Morning Show,' an entertainment-news-music series ... [which] will offer joshing by Walter Cronkite and a pair of puppets—'Humphrey, the Houn' Dog' and 'Charlemane, the Lion.' ... The character of 'The Morning Show' was in the process of being molded by many hands and minds one afternoon last week during a rehearsal in a studio in the Grand Central Terminal Building.... Mr. Cronkite took a seat on a high stool in front of a camera that had a Teleprompter attached. The first line of script in the Teleprompter read: 'I'm Walter Cronkite. Good Morning.'"
—*NEW YORK TIMES*, MARCH 14, 1954

6 Ginger Stanley on CBS News' *The Morning Show*, in Studio 41 at Grand Central, in 1955, the year she set a record by swimming seven miles underwater. *CBS Photo Archive, Getty Images*

7 In the control room of a CBS studio, 1939. *CBS Photo Archive, Getty Images*

8 CBS studio in 1946, during the filming of an amateur juvenile boxing match. *CBS Photo Archive, Getty Images*

"C.B.S.-TV apparently is going to blubber its weather forecasts on 'The Morning Show' from 7 to 8 A.M. beginning Tuesday. Meteorological data will be posted on the side of a specially built tank by Ginger Stanley, who will swim under water during the presentation."

—*NEW YORK TIMES*, NOVEMBER 19, 1955

9

Tennis Courts: "From actors to top tennis pros"

After CBS moved its studios out of the Terminal, the Vanderbilt Tennis Club opened two tennis courts in the same space. By 1980, Donald Trump had won the concession, operating the courts as a discreet athletic refuge for the famous. In 2009, the courts closed and were converted into a break room for train conductors, but a new lessor has now brought tennis back to the space, and revived the tennis club's original name.

9   The tennis courts in the Terminal, 2009.
Photograph by Frank English

PUBLIC NOTICE
TWO TENNIS COURTS
AT
GRAND CENTRAL
TERMINAL

METROPOLITAN TRANSPORTATION AUTHORITY is interested in leasing to a qualified firm or firms the operation of the tennis court facility in Grand Central Terminal. The facility which has approximately 23,177 square feet on three floors contains two full size tennis courts; shower, locker and sauna rooms; lounge area; offices and additional space for other use. Expressions of interest in negotiating such a lease will be entertained from principals with at least three years experience in the management of tennis court facilities or who propose to manage the operation through a firm having such experience

The sole purpose of this notice is to obtain expressions of interest in negotiating a lease as described above. METROPOLITAN TRANSPORTATION AUTHORITY makes no commitment by this notice to enter into such lease, reserves the right, in its sole discretion, to select those firms or firm with which to negotiate, or to elect not to negotiate with any firm.

Qualifying firms should submit no later than May 24, 1976, verified financial statements, annual reports (if available), a summary of their pertinent experience and such other data as may be relevant to:

STANLEY A. LEWIS
DIRECTOR OF REAL ESTATE

METROPOLITAN TRANSPORTATION AUTHORITY
1700 Broadway
New York, New York 10019   10

10 Ad reprinted from *New York Times*, April 20, 1976. Donald Trump leased the space for thirty years, attracting such stars as Robert Duvall and Dustin Hoffman, and tennis pros like John McEnroe, and Serena and Venus Williams.

Grand Central Theatre: "A theater of playing card size"

In 1937, a group of investors, led by John Sloan of the architectural firm Sloan & Robertson (designers of the Chanin Building on the southwest corner of 42nd Street and Lexington Avenue), opened a tiny theater in the Terminal, just opposite track 17, in the Graybar Passage. Built by Fred T. Ley & Co. (not by Sloan & Robertson), it advertised itself as "The Most Intimate Theatre in America" showing "UP-TO-THE-MINUTE NEWSREELS" along with "press scoops ... cartoons ... newest short subjects ... Major companies' previews. News Added As It Occurs." The theater ran continuous showings from nine A.M. to eleven P.M., and charged twenty-five cents per ticket.

The designers took special care to meet the needs of travelers, installing a large illuminated clock over an exit at the front—normally an unwanted annoyance in a dark theater. Gossip columnist Walter Winchell described the scene in 1939: "The travelers killing minutes before traintime in the Grand Central newsreel theatre.... Watching the films with one orb and the clock near the screen with the other...." Illustrator Tony Sarg adorned the walls of an adjoining "appointment lounge" with a mural showing a map of the world.

Sloan believed the theater to be the only one of its kind in the country. By 1966 it had become the last theater devoted exclusively to newsreels anywhere in New York. It survived into the 1970s, but closed by 1979. Renovations in 1997 uncovered a ceiling mural by Tony Sarg, visible now in the store occupying the space.

"A theatre of playing card size has accordingly been built in Grand Central Terminal.... Furthermore, though the programs will be comparatively brief, more traffic than in the ordinary theatre is expected in the aisles and between the rows; and the little auditorium, therefore, was planned with six inches of additional knee space for members of the audience. If John Jones, of Chicago, or Sam Smith, of New Rochelle, is leaving the theatre to catch the 6:15, you won't have to stand to let him go by.... Showing the completeness of the arrangements, there will be a private elevator for theatre patrons between the Upper and Lower Levels of the terminal."

—*WALL STREET JOURNAL*, MAY 4, 1937

"A new way to spend the longest hour in the world, the one that lies before you when you dash into Grand Central to find the gate of the 5:22 closing in your face and the next train leaving at 6:38, is rapidly being whipped into shape by a group of commuters and ex-commuters who kill time in a big way.... The progenitors of this capital idea are all men who have cooled their heels time after time in the vaulted loneliness of the Waiting Room watching the big clock tick off the interminable minutes that make up that never-ending hour referred to."

—*NEW YORK TIMES*, MAY 9, 1937

11 Grand Central Theatre ticket booth. *Courtesy of the Harry Ransom Center, the University of Texas at Austin*

12 A promotional postcard from the Grand Central Theatre. *Courtesy of the Theatre Historical Society Archives*

GRAND CENTRAL THEATRE Air Conditioned New York City

1 Grand Central Terminal, New York City
2 Part of the world-famous murals
3 America's most intimate theatre, with a clear view from any seat
4 The famous appointment lounge, designed by Tony Sarg
5 Main entrance, opposite Track 17

"A lady and four pieces of baggage were lugged out of the Grand Central newsreel theater at an early hour this morning. The lady was found wandering up the aisle in her nightgown looking for the washroom. She had boarded the theater by mistake, thinking it was the Boston sleeper."
—*BROOKLYN DAILY EAGLE*, APRIL 12, 1937

"The theatre interior is as complete a departure from the prevailing motif in cinema houses as one could hope for. The walls are of simple knotted pine, splayed out every third board or so in order to eliminate echoes. They are backed by acoustical plaster. Audiences enter from the side. In the rear, under the projection booth, is, of all things, an inglenook, with an unpretentious fireplace and room for a couple of easy chairs or seventy standees."
—*NEW YORK TIMES*, MAY 9, 1937

"The theatre is ... designed for a meeting place as well as for entertainment during waits for trains. The atmosphere is that of a well appointed living room rather than conventional theatre pattern. There is comfortable period furniture ... agreeable rugs and home-style lighting.... The 'bowled' architecture of Grand Central Theatre is a reflection in reduced proportions of the design of the newer type of outdoor sport stadium, where the spectator can look over instead of between the heads of those in front."
—*WALL STREET JOURNAL*, MAY 4, 1937

13 The tiny auditorium of the newsreel theater. *Photo Credit: SuperStock*

"Mr. Sarg was ... watching his favorite mural hanger cover the walls [of the lounge at the Grand Central Theatre] with Sargian projections of the world, with the accent on Manhattan. We heard Mr. Sarg tell the painter, 'Paint the ceiling a flat sky blue, and some time tomorrow I'll come around and paint the stars on it myself.' This area, or breathing space, will be called the Tony Sarg appointment lounge. Here people who have missed trains may pause and catch their breath.... Mr. Sarg's illustrated mural cartography is completely without political significance, unless his insistence on droshkies in Russia and chain gangs in Siberia can stir up a protest. Spain, for example, has a bull fighter and an ox-cart to illustrate it; England has a paunchy fellow in knee breeches, and Scotland has a donkey, after Doctor Johnson. We wondered what he'd do with Ethiopia, and searched around for Africa, but a very necessary doorway (it leads to the ladies' room) had interfered, ending Africa somewhere around Egypt...."

—*NEW YORK TIMES*, MAY 9, 1937

"Times change, and the production of short subjects that were once a staple of all movie house bills are in short supply, but the Grand Central Theatre carries on. It has been four years or so since the last newsreel for theatrical use was produced. But cartoons can still be found, as well as travelogues.... The neatly maintained theater has a changing audience: a lunchtime crowd of businessmen, salesmen and a scattering of secretaries, and an evening crowd, generally older, often residents of Tudor City or Murray Hill, who share a love of travel and find the Grand Central Theatre a comfortable place to review old favorites or size up the possibilities of a new vacation spot.... The charge at all times is one dollar."

—*NEW YORK TIMES*, AUGUST 29, 1972

Remodeling has overtaken one of the world's most unusual theatres, that within the Grand Central railroad terminal in New York. Originally installed 23 years ago as a newsreel theatre, it latterly changed to an hour's program of shorts, primarily for people waiting for trains. Sketched above is how the entrance will appear with remodeling completed. Drew Eberson, New York, is the architect.

14

15

14 Changes come to Grand Central Theatre. *Reprinted from* Motion Picture Herald, *January 14, 1961. Quigley Publishing Company. Courtesy of the Theatre Historical Society Archives.*

15 Tony Sarg's mural uncovered in the store currently occupying the theater space, 2012. Among his many accomplishments, Sarg originated the balloons in the annual Macy's Thanksgiving Day Parade. *Photograph by Frank English*

Grand Central Terminal's Post Office and Telegraph Office: "A wonderful assortment of elaborate machinery"

The trains that once connected Grand Central to cities across the country carried the mail along with the passengers, and the Grand Central Post Office dates back to the construction of the current Terminal. Though smaller than the main post office near Penn Station, it handled enormous quantities of mail and parcel post, and still processes much of the city's mail. Telegraph service dates even earlier, to the Depot, and a modern telegraph office continued that function in the new complex—back in an era that couldn't imagine e-mail and text messages for instant communication around the world.

"**The new Grand Central Terminal Railway Post-Office in New York, [is] equipped with a wonderful assortment of elaborate machinery for handling the mail…. On the main floor thousands of bags of mail are sorted by machinery. There is a system of belts that convey the bags all over the floor and finally to the chutes that lead into the side doors of the mail cars. When mail arrives at the terminal, it is placed on a mechanical device that lifts it to the top floor, where postal clerks sort it. Then the bags are dropped down to a raised platform and from there thrust onto the belts that carry them to other parts of the building, or to wagons or cars.**"

—*HERALD OF GOSPEL LIBERTY*, SEPTEMBER 16, 1915

"**With a small army of extra clerks and mail sorters … Postmaster Edward M. Morgan believes that he is equipped to handle and dispose of the enormous Christmas mail traffic successfully…. At the Grand Central Station … postal employes [sic] … have been working day and night, some of them with only a few hours' sleep. In addition to the local mails there were forty-three wagon loads of foreign mail from the steamships…. 30,000 bags of mail and parcel post matter were sent away yesterday. Some 15,000 bags were stacked in the baggage room, on the platforms and in the sorting rooms, which it was expected would be prepared for shipment to-day and the space cleared for the rush before Christmas.**"

—*NEW YORK TIMES*, DECEMBER 21, 1913

16 Sorting mail at the Grand Central Post Office, c. 1910. *Courtesy of the Library of Congress, Prints and Photographs Division*

17, 18 "Chuting" the mail, c. 1910. *Courtesy of the Library of Congress, Prints and Photographs Division*

19 The telegraph office in Grand Central Terminal, circa the 1940s. *Photograph by Edward O. Bagley*

20 The telegraph office in Grand Central Depot, 1896. *Courtesy of the Museum of the City of New York, Photo Archive Collection*

21 From the *Daily News*, May 23, 1946: "Railroad Strike ... Marianne Grande, of Asbury Park, New Jersey, due in Herkimer, New York, for her wedding, drops a 'See-you-soon, I hope' message to her fiance, in Grand Central Terminal." *Photograph by Bill Meurer/ NY Daily News Archive/Getty Images*

Soldiers and Sailors

The vast mobilization of soldiers for World War II brought more than a million young Americans—many for the first time in their lives—onto the country's trains and into its train stations. Grand Central found itself inundated with military travelers, often waiting in the Terminal for hours with nothing to do. In October 1942, the Travelers Aid Society of New York—which, since 1905, had operated a small desk near track 30, serving travelers in need—opened a servicemen's lounge in the Terminal, part of a chain of 120 such oases the Society planned around the country. The lounge occupied the east gallery, all 5,500 square feet of it, with a staff of some two hundred volunteers. According to the Society's director: "The purpose of the lounge will be to provide service men passing through the city a place of their own in which to relax, read and write. Our experience has shown that such a retreat is specially necessary, and specially welcomed, by service men who have several hours to kill between trains." The lounge stayed open only for the duration of World War II, closing in June of 1945. In 1948, the Society opened a marble booth on the north balcony, staffed by three social workers, and returned to its initial role aiding travelers in general, but the Terminal continued to host the military during peacetime.

"The color motif of the lounge will be carried out in red, white and blue.... Red will be employed at the north end, where there will be free checking facilities for clothing and equipment, two ping pong tables, two billiard tables, a piano and a mail box. The center section ... white, will be equipped as a library, with writing tables, sofas, books and magazines. The blue ... will have a snack bar and tables as well as two telephone booths, a bulletin board of amusements, another piano and a miniature motion picture machine."
—*NEW YORK TIMES*, OCTOBER 4, 1942

"During the war, Grand Central played host to countless servicemen and women. More than 2,000,000 troops traveled over the railroads of America each month. Many passed through the station en route overseas and returned later on their way home. These uniformed wayfarers often arrived lonely and weary.... The USO and Travelers Aid came to the rescue. A 'round-the-clock lounge was opened on the balcony above the concourse, where games were provided or where the tired soldier or sailor could curl up with a book, magazine or newspaper. A muted radio offered programs, and a canteen served coffee and sandwiches."
—*CORONET*, 1946

"In ten months more than 1,200,000 servicemen were guests of patriotic organizations active in the terminal. The Travelers Aid Society Lounge handles more than 100,000 a month. Men are given sleeping chairs, blankets and tags which state the time they are to be awakened. Cigarettes are free. Books and writing materials are furnished. Free billiard rooms are always open and entertainment includes movies and singing."
—*POPULAR MECHANICS*, NOVEMBER 1944

"National Guardsmen to Leave for Two Weeks in Field," July 8, 1955: "Thousands of troops will stream from home armories throughout the metropolitan area to Grand Central Terminal to entrain for [Camp Drum, near Watertown].... Tomorrow morning a truck convoy will leave the city with the division's supplies and equipment.... As in the past, the infantry units ... will spend most of the two weeks in the field."
—*NEW YORK TIMES*, JULY 8, 1955

22 Travelers Aid Society Lounge; the book collection is visible at the rear, c. 1942. *Courtesy of the Museum of the City of New York, Wurts Bros. Collection*

23 The 165th Regiment of the Rainbow Division in formation at Grand Central Terminal before boarding trains for camp, July 9, 1955. *Photograph by Judd Mehlman/NY Daily News Archive/Getty Images*

24 The canteen at the Travelers Aid Society Lounge, October 26, 1942. *Courtesy of the Museum of the City of New York, Wurts Bros. Collection*

25 Sailors waiting for a train, 1966. *Photograph by John Duprey/NY Daily News Archive/Getty Images*

Organ Concerts: "Organ music acts as a sedative for nerves"

Organ music

. . . and soloists and choirs were heard in many New York Central stations during the Christmas season. Marking her 25th consecutive year at the organ in Grand Central Terminal, Mary Lee Read directed a 21-day Yuletide music festival on the Terminal's north balcony. On the adjoining east balcony, the big Kodak colorama accented seasonal theme with a color picture of the boys' choir of Church of the Reformation in Rochester, N. Y.

26

If the vast Main Concourse suggests the soaring heights of a cathedral, what better instrument to fill the space with music than a grand organ? Starting on Christmas Day in 1928, Mary Lee Read, later billed as the Terminal's music director, played organ concerts from the balcony at Grand Central for close to thirty years. She first brought music to a train station in Denver; by 1943, the practice had spread to some twenty-three stations around the country. Ms. Read was particularly popular with servicemen during the war years.

26 Mary Lee Read at the organ in Grand Central. *Reprinted from the* New York Central Headlight, *1954.*

"Officials of the New York Central Railroad have found that organ music acts as a sedative for nerves jangled by the process of catching a train. 'The effect on fractious nerves,' they said, 'is apparent. Frowns fade, tension relaxes and all but the most case-hardened commuters step blithely to their trains. The great concourse proves to be a magnificent organ chamber, and yesterday thousands of transients halted in the waiting room and listened raptly to the harmonies.'"
—*NEW YORK TIMES*, MARCH 24, 1937

"'Oh, there you are—still playing the organ. It sure sounds good. Remember me?' And at the eager voice Mrs. Mary Lee Read looks up quickly from the keys of the organ on the balcony at Grand Central Station and smiles into the eyes of some lad in the armed forces who, after months at the front, returns on a fleeting furlough.... And so it has been day in and day out for Mary Lee Read

ever since she reached the happy conclusion that music should be as welcome in railroad stations as anywhere else, and proceeded to get it there. Now with hands and heart she plays two programs a day on the organ in Grand Central Station. Her music seems particularly to search out the weary, the lonely and far-from-home boys in the armed forces. Singly and in crowds they stand about the organ on the balcony of this bustling railroad terminal and join in singing or just listen.... One of the boys remarked that the music made the vast station seem somehow just like home."
—*CHRISTIAN SCIENCE MONITOR*, DECEMBER 24, 1943

"It had been touch-and-go, but Mrs. Mary Lee Read was back for her twenty-ninth season on the organ. Mrs. Read hadn't been feeling very well and wasn't sure she could make it. But there she was."
—*NEW YORK TIMES*, DECEMBER 11, 1956

The Oyster Bar: "An oyster stew that is famous throughout the country"

"For many ardent enthusiasts the oyster season will open tomorrow with breakfast at the Grand Central Terminal oyster bar. This establishment starts serving the succulent shellfish at what may seem an unearthly hour—6 A.M. But taking into account experience in previous years and recent inquiries, the manager predicts a full house as soon as the doors are unlocked—or almost."

—*NEW YORK TIMES*, AUGUST 31, 1950

LUNCH ROOM AND RESTAURANT, GRAND CENTRAL TERMINAL, NEW YORK.
WARREN & WETMORE AND REED & STEM, ASSOC. ARCHITECTS. Copyright, 1913. Tebbs-Hymans, I.

27

Architecture March 1913

None of Grand Central's other restaurants, large and small, can touch the Oyster Bar for its age, its fame, or its dramatic vaults. The Terminal's architects designed the restaurant space as part of their original plan. Though the restaurant served oysters from the beginning, it gained the name Oyster Bar only later, beginning life as the Grand Central Terminal Restaurant. Initially run by the Union News Company—an operator of restaurants around the country and newsstands throughout the Terminal—it became known as the Union News Restaurant, before taking on the name Mendel's Restaurant, after William H. Mendel, who, according to the *New-York Tribune* in 1913, had "for a great many years held the lease in the old Grand Central Station of the parcel room, cafe and lunch rooms." Mendel ran the restaurant until his death in 1918—at which time he "operated three restaurants, a confectionary store, a soda fountain and a toy shop at Grand Central Terminal." Members of his family continued the business.

The restaurant became a favorite of New Yorkers famous and obscure. In the 1930s, the society pages chronicled a number of "progressive parties"—sort of a restaurant crawl—which started at or included the Oyster Bar. Management changed several times over the decades, and some of the restaurant's original ornament disappeared. A major electrical fire in 1997 wreaked enormous damage, but a thorough restoration that same year brought the restaurant back to its original splendor.

27 The Terminal Restaurant in 1913, as illustrated in *Architecture* magazine. *Courtesy of the Picture Collection, the New York Public Library, Astor, Lenox and Tilden Foundation*

"Sights for sightseers in the biggest city in the world: Charles M. Schwab, chairman of the board, Bethlehem Steel corporation, perched on a stool at the Grand Central station oyster bar, eating stew."

—*ATLANTA CONSTITUTION*, MAY 4, 1928

"The wife of the President-Elect went to the restaurant of the Union News Company on the lower level of the Grand Central Terminal. There she donned a chef's apron, dipped out soup from a huge kettle on the kitchen range and served it at the first meal given by the company to a group of unemployed who have applied for assistance at the Travelers Aid Society and the Department of Public Welfare. On Mrs. Roosevelt's arrival at the restaurant, Mrs. Floyd G. Blair ... presented a bouquet to her.... Mrs. Roosevelt dropped a coin in one of the 'A Dime-in-Time' tin boxes and then went to the kitchen to serve the soup."

—*NEW YORK TIMES*, DECEMBER 2, 1932

28 Oyster Bar, 1974. *Photograph*: the New York Times

29 The oyster bar at the Oyster Bar. *Photograph by Gina Herold*

30 Eleanor Roosevelt, wife of newly elected president Franklin D. Roosevelt, serving soup to the unemployed at the Oyster Bar during the Depression. *Courtesy of the FDR Library*

"For some years the travelling salesman had seen former President Taft breakfasting at the table next [to] his own several times a week, when the present Chief Justice held the Kent Chair of International Law at Yale. The scene was that favorite haunt of commuters and early travellers, Mendel's Restaurant in Grand Central. A genial soul was the former President, replying affably to his waitress' gum-choked efforts at small talk."
—*NEW YORKER,* AUGUST 8, 1925

"The Grand Central Terminal Restaurant is in all respects one of the most up-to-date institutions, as to neatness, systematic and prompt service, rich furnishings with punctuality of employees so apparent that it is commented upon by all the regular patrons, and the many thousands of visitors, who throng the place daily.... The kitchen, with its up-to-date equipment, is in charge of one of the most able chefs obtainable, viz. Mr. Victor Keifer, formerly with the New York Athletic Club, and many first-class hotels. He is an artist, who knows how to cater to the taste of the most fastidious gourmet, and to please the palate of delicate epicureans. He has a staff, of forty-five persons including four first-class chefs, with all the necessary cooks, pastrymen, etc."
—*RAILROAD REPORTER AND TRAVELERS' NEWS,* FEBRUARY 1913

"Off early to gymnasium, where I did do my exercises and play at handballe [sic], descending afterwards to the Grand Central Station, which has become a new and hitherto unexplored playground for me. Lord! I did never dream that so many fascinating articles could be procured under one roof and without crossing any streets.... The men at the oyster bar are now numbered amongst my most pleasant acquaintances, and the minute they do see me approaching, one of them starts to mix a clam juice cocktayle [sic]."
—*LIFE,* "MRS. PEP'S DIARY," NOVEMBER 23, 1928

31 Cartoon featuring the Oyster Bar by George Shellhase, which originally appeared in *Ford Times,* February 1953. *Rod Kennedy Postcard Collection*

"That internationally famous Oyster Bar in Grand Central Station, New York City. There, two levels below the street, this oyster stew has been made by one recipe, by the hundreds of bowlfuls daily for 30 years.

Oyster Bar Stew
1 ½ dozen medium-sized oysters
¼ cup butter
salt and pepper to taste
dash of cayenne
¼ teaspoon paprika
celery salt to taste
dash Worcestershire sauce
1 cup clam broth
1 quart milk or cream

Carefully pick over oysters, removing bits of shell

and reserve liquor. Have top of the double boiler hot, hot. Add butter which should melt instantly. Add seasonings, then the shucked oysters, and stir until they come to a froth. Add clam broth and oyster liquor. Boil hard for a moment. Add milk, or cream or half and half, and boil up again. The oysters are now hot all the way through, but still tender. Immediately pour into warmed bowls. Add a pat of butter to float. Sprinkle with paprika. Serve with oyster crackers. Yield: 6 servings of stew divine."
—*ATLANTA CONSTITUTION*, SEPTEMBER 3, 1944

"Here 25,000 oysters are dispersed every day during the 'R' season, which brings the total for the eight-month period to approximately 10 million bivalves."
—*LOS ANGELES TIMES*, DECEMBER 18, 1949

"At a single terminal oyster bar, 15,000 oysters and 11,000 clams may be served in a day."

—*POPULAR MECHANICS*, NOVEMBER 1944

32 Advertisement for the Union News Restaurant, 1950s.

"The fabled Oyster Bar and Restaurant at Grand Central Terminal, where generations of harried commuters, world travelers, shoppers and midtown workers mingled under vaulted tile ceilings for seafood with a dash of bustling New York, was all but destroyed in a roaring fire early yesterday. Fire officials said the flames turned the restaurant on the lower level of the terminal into an inferno, melting down kitchen equipment and furnishings, bringing down hundreds of ceiling tiles and blackening the sprawling dining room, the wood-paneled saloon and a room with long serpentine marble counters where patrons for decades had sat elbow-to-elbow on stools for quick lunches."

—*NEW YORK TIMES*, JUNE 30, 1997

"His majesty the oyster is indigenous to this city and New Yorkers insist there are no oysters better than the fat firm Long Island kind, no dish to beat oyster stew as it's made at Grand Central Terminal. Here come the oyster lovers from all over the world. Stop at the bar any time day or night and you might see Lily Pons, for she likes to go there; so does Gene Tunney; so does Bing Crosby and Governor Tom Dewey and Mae West and Jim Farley. So does everyone who comes to town hungry for oysters."

—*LOS ANGELES TIMES*, DECEMBER 18, 1949

33 The Oyster Bar after the 1997 fire. *Photograph by Frank English*

34 The Oyster Bar in 2012. *Photograph by Frank English*

The Campbell Apartment: "The restoration and renovation of Grand Central Terminal has turned up a treasure"

"We've often heard of the office of Mr. John W. Campbell, but only the other day did we get into it. It's right in the Grand Central station; commuters rush by it every day without dreaming there's such an office there.... There's a small anteroom and then, bang: the office de luxe. It's sixty feet long, thirty wide; the ceiling is twenty-five feet above you. At a huge carved desk at the far end of the room sits Mr. Campbell, looking tiny. There is a pipe organ with three thousand pipes in the wall at his right, a piano at his left; Mr. Campbell can make them play, either alone or together, by pushing buttons on his desk. He usually has one or both going."
—*NEW YORKER*, JULY 9, 1932

The Campbell Apartment may be one of the most unusual rooms in Manhattan. John W. Campbell, chairman of the board of the Credit Clearing House of New York—which later merged with Dun & Bradstreet—leased the space from the New York Central in the early 1920s and hired architect Augustus N. Allen to turn it into an Italian Renaissance fantasy. In a typically 1920s burst of eclectic fervor, Allen jumbled together various sources, from medieval leaded-glass windows to a Renaissance-style painted wood ceiling to a grand balcony with Gothic quatrefoils. Campbell then draped the room with Persian rugs from his collection—said to be the best in the country—and filled it with six-foot-tall vases, bronze sculptures of horses (and one of his dog), seashell ashtrays, petrified tree trunks, and many other oddities. Though Campbell used the room only as an office, he did install a small kitchen, and often hosted evening musical entertainments with "well-known organists."

Campbell kept the office until the 1950s, but eventually Metro-North turned it into an office for its railroad police—and its wine cellar into a holding pen. Sheetrock, dropped ceilings, and fluorescent lights effectively banished Campbell's fantasy, until a 1997 restoration brought it back in all its varied brilliance.

"The restoration and renovation of Grand Central Terminal has turned up a treasure. A suite of rooms on the Vanderbilt Avenue side of the building that was decorated like a Florentine palazzo and for years was hidden behind the Sheetrock and fluorescent fixtures of the Metropolitan Transportation Authority offices, is slowly emerging from the dust. By next year, it will be an elegant lounge serving casual food."
—*NEW YORK TIMES*, NOVEMBER 26, 1997

35 John W. Campbell. *Courtesy of Elsie Fater*

36 Campbell's office, 1920s. *Courtesy of the Warren & Wetmore Collection, Avery Architectural & Fine Arts Library, Columbia University*

37 Painted wood ceiling, Campbell Apartment, New York City; Augustus N. Allen, c. 1923. *Photograph by Frank English, 2012*

38 The Campbell Apartment, converted for use by the Metro-North police, 1986. *Photograph by Frank English*

39 Painted wood ceiling, *Camera della Duchessa*, the Duchess's chamber, Palazzo Altemps, Rome; late fifteenth century.

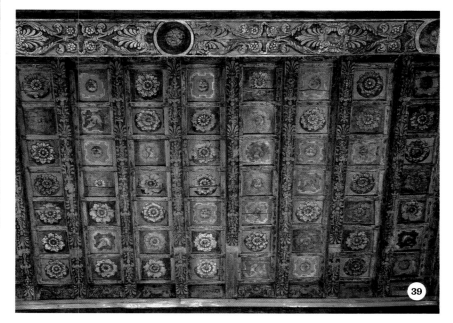

"The room is Italian Renaissance, from the colored beams in the ceiling (which painters lay on their backs for months painting) on down. Chairs carved with ducal crowns and coats of arms stand around.... Mr. Campbell ... is modest and reticent about his office. Says he just likes to have things around; no other point to it."

—*NEW YORKER*, JULY 9, 1932

Grand Central Market: "This New York equivalent of a European food hall"

"If you happen to come up from the Lexington Avenue subway line in the right part of Grand Central Terminal, you will walk into the train station's biggest surprise. Under the lights of 5,000 shimmering Austrian crystals suspended from a sculpture in the form of an olive tree are two fresh-fish stands, a cheese market, a spice bazaar, a greengrocer, a butcher shop, a bakery and six other small food stalls. In this New York equivalent of a European food hall, glistening oysters sit on chipped ice ... spicy aromas waft ... 350 domestic and imported cheeses are on display.... In a city with no shortage of dazzling marketplaces, Grand Central is still unique, with independent vendors grouped together, each with its own cash register."
—*NEW YORK TIMES*, DECEMBER 22, 1999

From the beginning, the Terminal hosted restaurants and food stores. One of its newest food purveyors, the Grand Central Market, opened in 1999 in 7,400 square feet of space just off Lexington Avenue and the Lexington Passage—a newly created corridor parallel to the Graybar Passage. Inside the Market, a dozen independent stores operate underneath a crystal chandelier that mimics an olive tree; its designer, Donald Lipski, named it "Sirshasana" after a yoga pose.

40 Charles Store, Grand Central, c. 1917. *Courtesy of the Museum of the City of New York, Wurts Bros. Collection*

41 The five thousand crystal "olives" of Sirshasana dangle over shoppers at Grand Central Market, c. 2000. *Photograph by Frank English*

Grand Central at the Movies

As one of the best-known and most inherently dramatic locations in New York, over the decades Grand Central has served as a film set, being featured in several dozen films, including: *Going Hollywood*, with Bing Crosby and Marion Davies (1933); *Twentieth Century*, with Carol Lombard and John Barrymore (1934); *Spellbound*, with Gregory Peck and Ingrid Bergman (1945); *Ma and Pa Kettle Go to Town*, with Marjorie Main and Percy Kilbride (1950); *North by Northwest*, with Cary Grant and Eva Marie Saint (1958); and *Seconds*, with Rock Hudson (1966), as well as such blockbusters as *The Godfather* in 1972, the first *Superman* movie in 1978, and *The Fisher King*, with Jeff Bridges, in 1991. While Grand Central has brought the world to New York City, Hollywood has brought Grand Central to the world.

42, 43 The New York Central Board Room, in the New York Central Building, was used in *The Godfather* for the scene of the meeting of the Five Families. Portraits of William H. and Cornelius Vanderbilt flank the fireplace. *Photograph of* The Godfather: mptvimages.com

"Alfred Hitchcock arrived here last night to prepare for the New York phase of his production of 'North by Northwest,' the suspense drama he will film for Metro-Goldwyn-Mayer. Cary Grant and Eva Marie Saint, the film's stars, are scheduled to take part in the location shooting in Manhattan."

—*NEW YORK TIMES*, AUGUST 22, 1958

"Anyone spying on the location work Alfred Hitchcock has been doing here for the last two weeks on his suspense drama 'North by Northwest' might have had the uneasy feeling that he was privy to an ultra-secret operation, knowledge of which constituted automatic aid and comfort to the enemy. The presence of the legion of Metro-Goldwyn-Mayer technicians and Cary Grant, the film's star, was anything but a secret, as curious crowds gathered wherever the film people went to work [including] Grand Central Terminal."

—*NEW YORK TIMES*, SEPTEMBER 7, 1958

44 Cary Grant hiding in plain sight in *North by Northwest,* 1958.

45 Gregory Peck and Ingrid Bergman at Grand Central in Alfred Hitchcock's *Spellbound. Photo Credit: mptvimages.com*

46 A film crew sets up a shot on the Main Concourse in 1986 for *The House on Carroll Street,* a film about McCarthyism, set in New York in 1951 (the photographer is facing the Pan Am Building entrance and the North Balcony). Trains were rerouted to the lower level for the day's filming. *Photograph by Frank English*

47 Alfred Hitchcock filming *North by Northwest* at the
Terminal, 1958. *Photograph by Phil Greitzer/NY Daily
News Archive/Getty Images*

8

NEW YORK'S TOWN SQUARE

Every week, from the 1930s to the 1950s, radios brought the daily drama of Grand Central into living rooms across the country. Every day, thousands of passengers and passersby walked through the Terminal. As the largest, grandest, and most famous public space in the city, Grand Central naturally became the place where thousands of New Yorkers gathered—to cheer on returning victorious teams, to watch the spectacle of the first rocket launches of the American space program, to celebrate New Year's Eve. With so many people constantly coming and going, the Terminal offered an unmatched audience for exhibitions, for performances, and of course for advertisements. And on a more somber note, it offered space for memorials. Though Terminal City never became the civic center imagined in the earliest plans, Grand Central became New York's de facto town square.

"Grand Central Station! Crossroads of a million private lives! Gigantic stage on which are played a thousand dramas daily!"
—OPENING OF THE RADIO DRAMA *GRAND CENTRAL STATION*

"It's a railway terminal, of course; but it's also a kind of crossroads at the heart and center of New York. It's known to everybody, open to everybody; and its splendid Concourse is everybody's meeting place. 'I'll see you at the Golden Clock at Grand Central.' ... You heard [these words], sometimes, in the mouths of people who had never been to America, but who understood that, once arrived, they could surely find each other beside the four-faced Golden Clock at Grand Central Station."
—*GRAND CENTRAL*, DAVID MARSHALL,1946

1 *Photograph by Frank English*

2

"About 260,000,000 pairs of feet took billions of steps in one of the most famous buildings in the world during the past year, yet few caught more than a hasty, passing glimpse of the remarkable structure which is busier than many cities. The structure is Grand Central Terminal in New York City…. In a recent day more than 230,000 train passengers entered and left Grand Central Terminal. At least 600,000 other people, non-passengers, hurried through the Terminal's concourses and subterranean passages in the course of their business day."
—*POPULAR MECHANICS*, NOVEMBER 1944

"The number of people who pass through Grand Central in a year approximate the total population of the United States."
—*WPA GUIDE TO NEW YORK CITY*, 1939

"There are several million phone booths in the world today but this one is the busiest one anywhere. Bringing in 12 times as much revenue as the average public telephone booth, it is used by more than 300 people daily. That works out to better than one call every five minutes, around the clock."
—*CHRISTIAN SCIENCE MONITOR*, OCTOBER 30, 1964

2 The morning rush. *Photograph by Frank English*

3 Some ten thousand fans descended on the Terminal in 1941 to welcome home the Brooklyn Dodgers after they won the National League pennant in Boston. *Photograph © Bettmann/CORBIS*

4 New Year's Eve, 1963, a benefit for the National Association for Mental Health, which leased the space for the occasion. Train travel was not affected. *Courtesy of the* New York Times

5 A new New Year's Eve tradition: First Night, 1993. *Photograph by Frank English*

Celebrations

The Terminal has seen many celebrations. Some were a natural result of train arrivals or departures, as when baseball fans deluged the Terminal to celebrate returning champions. When the New York Giants won the National League championship in September 1933, ten thousand fans met the triumphantly returning team at the Terminal. Almost as many Dodger fans flooded the Concourse in 1941. In more recent times, enormous parties at the Terminal have welcomed in the New Year.

"The jubilant rooters took complete command of the station to extend a roaring welcome to Manager Leo Durocher and his men.... This hastily arranged celebration lured fans from all sections of the borough. Smiling merchants and happy youngsters, politicians and plumbers, taxi drivers and street car motormen—all were there for the single purpose of honoring the Flatbush heroes."
—*NEW YORK TIMES*, SEPTEMBER 26, 1941

"The vaulted main concourse of Grand Central Terminal became a ballroom last night where 1,500 persons danced in the New Year. The occasion was the first Bell Ringer Ball, sponsored by the National Association for Mental Health.... The dancers, in dinner jackets and long gowns, spun on the freshly mopped marble floor. Festoons of thousands of balloons hung from the ceiling.... At midnight, as Guy Lombardo and his orchestra played 'Auld Lang Syne,' the balloons were released and fell in a cascade of red, blue, green and yellow."
—*NEW YORK TIMES*, JANUARY 1, 1964

"It may look like the minutelong waltz scene from 'The Fisher King' or a certain bubbly evening with Guy Lombardo in the 1960's, but it will be a first, not a rerun: a night of waltzing in Grand Central Terminal, the centerpiece of a new kind of New Year's celebration."
—*NEW YORK TIMES*, DECEMBER 26, 1991

Exhibitions

"Before a crowd of 17,000, one of the largest ever assembled in Grand Central Terminal, Mayor Walker and Colonel James C. Fitzmaurice unveiled the veteran Junkers all-metal monoplane Bremen yesterday afternoon at 3 o'clock.... The unveiling was preceded by a luncheon at the Hotel Commodore, attended by [transatlantic aviators including] Amelia Earhart.... The late Baron Guenther von Huenefeld donated it to the people of the city of New York in appreciation of the reception tendered to him and his crew on their completion of [their historic flight]."

—*NEW YORK TIMES*, MAY 22, 1929

6

Grand Central has always had a role in exhibitions of all kinds. In the late nineteenth and early to mid-twentieth centuries, most of these were hosted by the adjoining Grand Central Palace, especially automobile and flower shows. The Grand Central Galleries played a major role in the city's art world. But the Terminal itself has hosted a variety of exhibits—everything from public health displays to fashion shows.

In 1916, the City displayed a model of proposed improvements to Riverside Park, then a subject of some controversy. In 1918, the American Museum of Natural History, with the New York State Food Commission, mounted a food conservation exhibit in the east gallery, illustrating "an ideal diet." In December of 1931, in the north balcony, Bishop William Manning inaugurated a display of a twelve-and-a-half-foot-long detailed model of the Cathedral Church of Saint John the Divine, illustrating how the Cathedral would look upon completion. In October 1934, New York State mounted an exhibit of one thousand photos illustrating various work relief projects providing employment for victims of the Depression. In September 1935, the state sponsored a yearlong exhibit on the east balcony promoting the state's tourism wonders—including scenes of Lake Placid in the snow, Jones Beach in the summer, and a "musical waterfall" representing Watkins Glen State Park. In June 1948, the New Haven Railroad and Filene's department store of Boston put on a fashion show on the balcony, which included importing 1,000 square feet of sand from Cape Cod to create a beach for models in bathing suits.

In recent years, the former Main Waiting Room was renamed Vanderbilt Hall, devoted to art and trade exhibitions and craft fairs. But decades earlier, Kodak had its own exhibition hall in the Terminal—the Kodak Photographic Information Center on the east balcony—which hosted among many others a 1951 one-man show of Edward Weston's work, a 1953 show of night photography, a 1954 show on the history of photography, and a 1962 show of "Sportsmen in Action."

Armaments have also been displayed: a twenty-two-foot-long model of the *Shangri-La* aircraft carrier of the Seventh Fleet on the Main Concourse in 1955, and an eighteen-foot scale model of the Sergeant, a solid-fuel missile, displayed in May 1958 to mark Armed Forces Week.

But perhaps most memorable of recent exhibits was the extraordinary fantasy of Red Grooms's *Ruckus Manhattan,* in Vanderbilt Hall, which recast the Terminal as a grand exhibition space.

"The exhibit, known as 'Main Street, Southern New England' ... [has] a full-scale model of a colonial village beside a display of the products of New England. Exhibits ... include the press on which Benjamin Franklin learned to print ... the post-office where P.T. Barnum called for his mail, an old apothecary shop, a cobbler's shop and the oldest marionette theatre in America."

—*NEW YORK TIMES*, FEBRUARY 18, 1948

6 The crowd of seventeen thousand assembled to watch the unveiling of the Bremen airplane on May 21, 1929. *Photograph © Bettmann/CORBIS*

7 The Bremen, which made the world's first nonstop flight, east to west, across the North Atlantic, on display over the east balcony, 1929. It hovers above the DeWitt Clinton train, in 1831 the first to carry passengers in New York State. Both plane and train were part of a transportation exposition at the Terminal. *Photograph © Bettmann/CORBIS*

8 Both versions of the Grand Central Palace regularly hosted automobile shows. Since then, displays of individual autos have often been seen in the Terminal.

40-Year Bolshevik Record Shown at Grand Central

THE CLASSLESS SOCIETY

Nathaniel Block, a merchant seaman, pauses before photo of Stalin at the new exhibit

"In New York the Redstone missile of the U.S. Army and the largest operational weapon of its kind in the free world poked its shiny nose up toward the ceiling of Grand Central Terminal. It was being displayed for three weeks as a salute to International Geophysical Year. It weighs five tons, is 63 feet tall and required two days' work by 14 men to set it up."

—*LIFE*, JULY 22, 1957

"A pictorial exhibit of Bolshevism's forty-year record, portraying 'the grim Soviet reality in its true colors,' was opened yesterday in the lower-level lobby of Grand Central Terminal. The collection of enlarged photographs, maps and textual material was prepared by the Assembly of Captured European Nations.... Senator Jacob K. Javits and Countess Alexandra Tolstoy formally opened the exhibit."

—*NEW YORK TIMES*, JANUARY 21, 1958

9 The Redstone missile on display at the Terminal in 1957. *Photograph © Walter Sanders-*Life *Magazine-Getty Images*

10 An exhibit on the evils of Bolshevism comes to the Terminal in 1958, at the height of the Cold War. *Reprinted courtesy of the* New York Times, *January 21, 1958*

"A small city itself—fantastic, exaggerated, crazily angled and vividly hued—the 'Red Grooms at Grand Central' installation in the terminal's former waiting room would easily qualify as a milestone on its own. But officials see it as an opening act for something bigger. 'What Red Grooms should do is begin to bring people back to the terminal.... And as they look through the art, what they're seeing behind it is a restored space of a quality we'd like to see the whole terminal look like.' "

—*NEW YORK TIMES*, MARCH 7, 1993

11 Red Grooms at work, 1993.

12 *Ruckus Manhattan*, Red Grooms' fantasy portrayal of the island, installed in the Main Waiting Room in 1993. Visitors find out what all the ruckus is about.

13 In 1987, Dancing in the Streets organized "Grand Central Dances"—creating "a historic union of dance and architecture"—with works by choreographers like Merce Cunningham. Performances included juggling acts, laser beams, and dancing on the catwalks within the windows.

14 As part of "Grand Central Dances," Philippe Petit walked a tightrope high above the Main Concourse, 1987. *Photographs by Frank English*

Performances

"Fantastic. The Woodstock of the Eighties? 'Grand Central Dances'—a mammoth multimedia dance event staged in the nooks and crannies of Grand Central Terminal, on the vast expanse of its main concourse, within the walkways of its huge tiered windows and even in the air—just a few feet below the station's cavernous ceiling—will certainly remain a night to remember.... The whole thing was ... a very New York event."
—*NEW YORK TIMES*, OCTOBER 11, 1987

"Tonight's show will end as Mr. Petit—the man who walked a tightrope between the tops of the two World Trade Center towers in 1974—will stride across a wire suspended beneath the 2,500 stars of the concourse's vaulted ceiling."
—*NEW YORK TIMES*, OCTOBER 9, 1987

Just as Grand Central Palace hosted exhibitions, it also hosted performances—but so has the Terminal proper, including a long-running annual concert of Christmas carols alternating with an organ recital. Highlights have included the 1935 performance by the Manhattan Concert Band—a Works Progress Administration project—featuring works by Berlioz, Mendelssohn, and Bizet, as well as the song "I've Been Working on the Railroad." In 1943, the Princeton Theological Seminary Choir performed an Easter concert. More recently, in 1998, on the east balcony, the Westchester Philharmonic played "Grand Central!"—a piece commissioned for the rededication of the Terminal—that evoked bursts of steam and the sound of train wheels on the rails. And in 2007, pianist Yefim Bronfman gave a morning concert to benefit the Food Bank for New York City, a few days before his more formal Carnegie Hall recital.

"Youngsters competing in the double-Dutch jump rope competition yesterday in the Grand Concourse at Grand Central Terminal. In two-minute spurts, they jumped two ropes simultaneously trying to skip more times than their counterparts. About 100 youngsters took part in the contest, which is part of the city-sponsored New York Summer Games."
—*NEW YORK TIMES*, AUGUST 23, 1988

"There once was a time when musicians, dancers and actors confined themselves mainly to theaters and concert halls.... But, in the age of outdoor happenings and offbeat 'performance spaces,' performers have seemingly usurped every conceivable nontheatrical nook and cranny.... Even Grand Central Terminal. Tonight and tomorrow, the venerable concourse turns into a magical, multidimensional state, where dancers will dazzle, lasers will sparkle and a high-wire artist will maneuver 100 feet above a melee of commuters."
—*NEW YORK TIMES*, OCTOBER 4, 1987

15 Double Dutch jump rope competition in the Main Concourse, August 1988. *Photograph by Frank English*

16 An exhibition of Rollerblading in the Main Concourse, 1992. *Photograph by Frank English*

Messages for The Millions

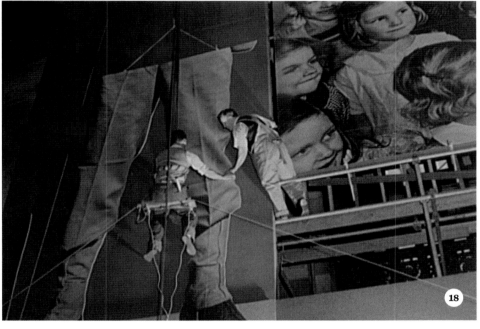

"The face of the 13¹/₂-foot illuminated clock in Grand Central Terminal has changed again, getting its sixth—and perhaps final—sponsor in more than two decades of conspicuous timetelling. Merrill Lynch is the latest, following Newsweek, Trans World Airlines, Manufacturers Hanover Trust Company, Newsweek (an earlier appearance) and Westclox, the original advertiser. In its new incarnation, the giant clock between the concourse and main waiting room has digital faces for London and Tokyo time and will give news and stock information on its running message board. Jason Perline, president of Van Wagner Communications, operators of the clock, also said that its long-silent chimes would be repaired and 'the sound of Big Ben will reverberate around Grand Central again.'"

—*NEW YORK TIMES*, AUGUST 11, 1986

Millions of people, waiting in a gigantic room: What a wonderful audience for advertisers! Today the Terminal has dispensed with the gaudiest advertisements, but once upon a time some of the city's largest and most noticeable displays hung on the walls of the Main Concourse.

17 The Merrill Lynch clock, 1988. As if Grand Central didn't have enough clocks, this enormous addition, almost as large as the Tiffany timepiece, hung over the entrance to the Main Concourse and gave commuters both the time and an advertising message, not to mention a replica of the chimes of London's Big Ben. *Photograph by Frank English*

18 In 1941, the U.S. government hung a vast mural—118 feet long by 100 feet high—over the east balcony, promoting defense bonds. *Photograph of the mural's installation by Edwin Rosskam. Courtesy of the Library of Congress Prints and Photographs Division*

"The world's largest photo-mural, symbolizing the defense of America and her traditions, was dedicated yesterday in the Grand Central Terminal with a stirring ceremony conducted under the auspices of the United States Treasury Department and attended by 3,000 persons.... Broadcast from coast to coast over the National Broadcasting Company's blue network, the ceremony was held on the main floor and mezzanine, where, at the east end, the huge mural stands 'for the duration,' towering to the arched ceiling."

—*NEW YORK TIMES*, DECEMBER 15, 1941

"A feature of the exhibit is the largest color transparency ever made, according to company officials. The photograph is eighteen feet high and sixty feet long and presents in three panels the picture of a mother photographing her little boy and girls, together with close-up pictures of them both. The giant photograph is known as the 'Kodak Colorama.' The transparency will be replaced with new pictures from time to time."
—*NEW YORK TIMES*, MAY 16, 1950

"A chapter of photography history is coming to an end.... Ever since I was a babe in arms, the city's most famous meeting spot has been brightened by a succession of huge, colorful images that have been installed by the world's most famous photography firm. It all began in 1949, and this month's entrant is number 565 in the series. It's also the last. After Dec. 30, the Colorama will be history."
—*NEW YORK TIMES*, DECEMBER 3, 1989

19 The Defense Bonds mural in place, 1941. *Photograph by Arthur Rothstein. Courtesy of the Library of Congress, Prints and Photographs Division.*

20 Perhaps the most eye-catching advertisement ever installed at Grand Central, the Kodak Colorama sign over the windows above the east balcony. *Photograph by Frank English, 1985*

21 Restoration of the Main Concourse offered extra-large spaces for advertisements, which largely disappeared from the restored Terminal. *Photograph by Frank English, c. 1998*

Sharing the News

"The thoughts of millions of New Yorkers were riveted for hours yesterday on one man alone in space.... The most spectacular display of interest occurred in Grand Central Terminal.... They began to arrive about 6:30 A.M. Their numbers swelled rapidly after 8 A.M. Just before the blast-off, Captain Frank Campbell of the railroad police estimated that 9,000 to 10,000 persons stood shoulder to shoulder, their faces turned like sunflowers to the screen."
—*NEW YORK TIMES*, FEBRUARY 21, 1962

"A capacity crowd of 8,000 jammed into the main concourse of Grand Central terminal yesterday to see on television the launching of Maj. L. Gordon Cooper Jr.... To view the oversize 12-by-16 foot screen ... the crowd overflowed onto stairways and balconies. The hubbub dwindled to silence as the countdown reached its final seconds, and then swelled to cheers and applause as the space capsule roared from its pad at 9:04 A.M. A hush fell again until the success of the shot was confirmed, and then the exodus to work and train began."
—*NEW YORK TIMES*, MAY 16, 1963

With so many people passing through the Terminal every day, Grand Central came to function as a grand public piazza where citizens could gather to share the news of the day. In particular, during the 1960s, thousands of New Yorkers flocked to the Terminal to watch the drama of countdowns and liftoffs during the early years of the space program. In 1970, New Yorkers held their breath while watching the splash down of the aborted *Apollo 13*, the doomed moon shot whose astronauts miraculously piloted the damaged ship back to earth.

GOVERNOR GETS ROUSING RECEPTION ON RETURN FROM CAMPAIGN TOUR

Mr. Lehman, accompanied by Mrs. Lehman, acknowledging the enthusiastic welcome. — *Times Wide World*   Part of the huge crowd that greeted Mr. Lehman as he arrived at the Grand Central station last night. — *Times Wide World*

> "In New York City, thousands watched the recovery [of Apollo 13] in the Pacific on a giant television screen above the old New Haven Railroad ticket windows in the upper level of Grand Central Terminal. There were nervous whispers of 'They've got this far at least,' and 'it's amazing.' Three times there was long, loud clapping—once when the space capsule appeared on the screen high in the sky, then when it splashed into the Pacific and again when the astronauts limped out."
>
> —*NEW YORK TIMES*, APRIL 18, 1970

22 Thousands gathered at the Terminal to watch John Glenn blast into orbit in 1962. *Photograph © Bettmann/CORBIS*

23 On a Main Concourse cluttered with advertising, including Kodak's newly organized Exhibit center, hundreds watch the launch of astronaut Gordon Cooper, May 16, 1963, on the CBS News monitor (far right). *Photograph by Frank Frattali*

Making the News

Politicians have often come through Grand Central to meet the voters. In 1923, thousands turned out to greet President Calvin Coolidge when he arrived at the Terminal. In 1924, another crowd welcomed Teddy Roosevelt, returning from an upstate campaign jaunt as he ran for governor. In 1938, they came for Governor Herbert Lehman. In May 1940, the supporters of presidential candidate Thomas Dewey "jammed" the Terminal, while in 1952 they came to see President Truman. In 1964, the headlines proclaimed "[Robert F.] Kennedy Mobbed in Grand Central." But perhaps no political event could match the spectacle of 1917: When the New York City delegates to the Labor Loyalty convention left Grand Central for Minneapolis, they were seen off by a crowd of five thousand supporters in an event directed by the Mayor's Committee on National Defense—complete with music from the Caledonian Pipers, a brass band, and opera singer Marie Louise Wagner standing at the west stairs singing the National Anthem.

The Terminal has also attracted political protests. In December 1967, antiwar protesters let fly fifteen doves in the Terminal—to the dismay of the ASPCA.

> "**Governor Lehman returned last night from his up-State campaign tour to be greeted at Grand Central Terminal by the biggest crowd and the most tumultuous reception he had received anywhere on his ten-day trip, which took him through Central and Northern New York. Obviously moved by the reception from the 'hometown' folks, the Governor halted briefly on the steps leading from the concourse of the station to the Vanderbilt Avenue exits to tell his welcomers that he expected an 'outstanding and sweeping victory for the Democratic ticket' on Nov. 8.**"
>
> —*NEW YORK TIMES*, OCTOBER 31, 1938

24 New York Governor Herbert Lehman returns to Grand Central from a campaign trip. *Photograph by Times Wide World*

"President Truman came charging into New York last night for the ninety-eighth stop on his two-week whistle-stop tour of the country by special train, continuing his appeal for the election of Gov. Adlai E. Stevenson of Illinois, Democratic candidate for President."

—*NEW YORK TIMES*, OCTOBER 11, 1952

"The organizers of the be-in—the Youth International Party—said they had planned the affair as a gathering of youths to share songs, popcorn, jellybeans and love for humanity. But the gathering became a disorderly rally in which the youths chanted anti-draft slogans and painted antiwar messages on the walls until they were shoved out of the terminal by wedges of police of the Tactical Patrol Force.... A little after 1 A.M., firecrackers began exploding over the heads of the police and the demonstrators. Then a band of youths climbed on the roof of the information booth and began spinning the hands of the four-faced clock."

—*NEW YORK TIMES*, MARCH 24, 1968

25 President Harry Truman at the Terminal in 1952, campaigning for his hoped-for successor in the White House.

26 Some of the estimated 3,000 Yippies at a "Yip-In," an anti–Vietnam War protest at the Terminal, mount the information desk in the Main Concourse, 1968. *Photo Credit: Copyright © Bettmann/CORBIS*

27

When the Lights Went Out

The blackout of 1965 affected the entire northeast of the country. New Yorkers famously helped each other get through the crisis. Grand Central Terminal hosted thousands of stranded commuters overnight.

"The Night the Power Failed will be recalled by the millions who lived through it as an eerie all-night fantasy when the whole machinery of life came to a halt.... Around midnight numbed commuters began seeking darkened recesses in the big station. Some sprawled on the floor in the waiting room; hundreds sat on the draughty, stalled escalators leading to the Pan Am building and tried to sleep."
—*NEW YORK TIMES*, NOVEMBER 11, 1965

"The men in the information booth at Grand Central were tired of answering inquiries about when the trains were going to run and merely shrugged.... Morale was bolstered for a time by a young lady who perched herself on the counter of the information booth and appealed for help in doing a crossword puzzle. 'I need a five letter word starting with "L" meaning "vertical column," ' she called out. Forty adults clustered nearby frowned in deep concentration."**
—*NEW YORK TIMES*, NOVEMBER 11, 1965

27 The blackout, 1965. Commuters spend the night at Grand Central Terminal during the northeast power failure that began at 5:27 P.M., November 9, 1965. While the large electric Westclox (later Merrill Lynch) clock stopped when the power failed, the information booth clock continued to run. *Photograph © The Granger Collection, New York*

28

In Memoriam

Grand Central has played host to many memorials. On November 11, 1922, as the city marked the newly declared Armistice Day, recalling the dead of World War I, a bugler on a balcony sounded "taps," and the usually noisy and hectic terminal fell silent for two minutes of prayer just before 11:00 A.M. When the body of Myron T. Herrick, the late U.S. ambassador to France, returned to New York in 1929, his funeral cortege was met at Grand Central by a crowd of ten thousand.

Perhaps most personal for Grand Central itself was the memorial held for Mrs. Jacqueline Kennedy Onassis, whose efforts ultimately kept the Terminal from destruction. Perhaps the most poignant was the impromptu memorial that evolved from the thousands of missing-person flyers posted following the attacks of September 11, 2001. Grand Central must have seemed the logical place for such messages—where else would they be seen by so many people?

"Commuters in busy Grand Central paused to watch a short film of King's biography and to listen to excerpts of King's memorable 'I Have a Dream' speech shown in the grand concourse sponsored by Metro North."
—*NEWSDAY*, JANUARY 20, 1987

"At the terminal yesterday, people from all over the world gathered in the newly restored South Hall to sign and scribble their feelings in a memorial book to Mrs. Onassis. Nearby, a spotlighted plaque read: 'Jacqueline Kennedy Onassis led the fight to save this beautiful terminal. The victory won in the United States Supreme Court in 1978 established the public's right to protect landmarks in cities and towns all over America.'"
—*NEW YORK TIMES*, MAY 22, 1994

28 New Yorkers celebrate Martin Luther King Jr. Day watching his "I Have a Dream" speech during a day-long screening in Grand Central's Main Concourse, January 18, 1987. *Photograph by Frank English*

29 Memorial to Jacqueline Kennedy Onassis, 1994. *Photograph by Steven Ahlgren*

30 In the immediate aftermath of the 9/11 attacks, people searching for friends and relatives posted notices around the Terminal. Metro-North then put up these message boards in the Lexington Passage to accommodate them. *Photograph by Frank English*

31

AFTERWORD

Grand Central Terminal has survived a turbulent history to see the beginning of its second century. Its rescue and stunning renovation rank as one of the great successes not just of the historic preservation movement, but also of the massive infusion of energy and resources that have restored the city's fortunes since their nadir in the 1970s. Grand Central today stands as a monument to New York's stature as a great world city.

Countless New Yorkers, from the famous and powerful to the unsung and unknown, worked tirelessly for many years to ensure Grand Central's survival and renewal. If the fate of its rival, Pennsylvania Station—a civic monument effectively tossed on a trash heap in the Jersey meadowlands—followed inevitably from a heedless worship of material progress all too typical of the city's life, then the Terminal's dramatic restoration is testament to a hard-headed, practical, but ultimately romantic attachment that New Yorkers have to their city. The revival of Grand Central reflects the city's dynamism, its determination to overcome any obstacle, every bit as much as Commodore Vanderbilt's empire building and William Wilgus's vision and imagination.

If we may adapt the inscription just inside the Terminal entrance beneath the Pershing Square Viaduct:

"To all those who with head, heart and hand toiled in the rebirth of this monument to the public service, this is inscribed."

31 *Photograph by Frank English, 2005*

BIBLIOGRAPHY

Adams, Val. "Morning TV: Gadgetry, Puppetry and News." *New York Times*, March 14, 1954: X13.

Allen, W.F. "The Reformation in Time-Keeping." *Scientific American Supplement*, vol. 18, December 20, 1884: 7472.

"All Lighted Up." *New Yorker*, February 9, 1929: 12.

"All the Way." *Chicago Daily Tribune*, August 25, 1957: F30.

American Architect and Building News, vol. 16, no. 466, November 29, 1884: 254.

American Architect and Building News, vol. 74, no.1350, November 9, 1901.

American Railway Times, December 4, 1858: 10.

Anderson, Susan Heller and Dunlap, David W. "Grand Central Clock Gets a Makeover." *New York Times*, August 11, 1986: B3.

"An Architectural Ramble." *Real Estate Record and Builder's Guide*, vol. 6, no. 131, September 17, 1870: 3.

"Architectural Iron-work." *American Architect and Building News*, vol. 16, no. 469, December 20, 1884: 298.

Arnold, Martin. "World Rejoices at Safe Return." *New York Times*, April 18, 1970: 1.

"Artists in Grand Central." *New York Times*, August 21, 1924: 10.

Art News, An International Newspaper of Art, March 17, 1923: 1.

"Art Patrons Draw Prizes at Exhibit." *New York Times*, November 24, 1933: 23.

"At the Grand Central Terminal." *Railway and Locomotive Engineering*, vol. 26, no. 3, March 1913: 86.

Bankers Magazine, January 1913: 38 ff.

Baury, Louis. "The Beaux Arts at the Front." *The Bookman: A Review of Books and Life*, October 1916: 113.

Bigart, Homer. "A Night of Confusion, Frustration and Adventure." *New York Times*, November 11, 1965.

"Big Lounge to Open in Grand Central." *New York Times*, October 4, 1942: 27.

Bowen, Stirling. "Movies While You Wait." *Wall Street Journal*, May 4, 1937: 15.

"Bremen Unveiled at Grand Central." *New York Times*, May 22, 1929: 12.

Brooklyn Daily Eagle, April 12, 1937: 9.

Brown, Christian. "8,000 Watch Shot in Grand Central." *New York Times*, May 16, 1963: 19.

Buckley, Thomas. "1,500 Celebrate in Grand Central." *New York Times*, January 1, 1964: 28.

Burros, Marion. "Grand Central's Little Secret: It's a Destination for Cooks." *New York Times*, December 22, 1999: F1.

"Buy Your Masterpieces Between Trains." *New York Times*, March 18, 1923: SM4.

"Celebrate the End of Elevated Spur; Two Associations Hold Parade and Luncheon Over 42d Street Improvement." *New York Times*, May 23, 1924.

"Central Now Plans a Wonderful Plaza: More Millions to Be Spent in Beautifying the New Grand Central Terminal." *New York Times*, March 4, 1910.

"Central Terminal Opening on Sunday: Men Working Day and Night to Finish Main Section of the Great Station." *New York Times*, January 29, 1913.

Childs, Kingsley. "10,000 Fans Pack Grand Central to Acclaim Returning Dodgers." *New York Times*, September 26, 1941: 29.

"City's New and Great Portal— Grand Central Terminal: Father Knickerbocker and his Children Have Reason to be Proud of this Monumental Acquisition." *New York Tribune*, December 15, 1912: B8.

"City under One Roof Extends Borders; Unique Grand Central Group, With Its Underground Connections, Becoming a Self-Sufficient Centre." *New York Times*, August 29, 1926.

"City." *New Yorker*, January 1, 1927: 8.

"Civic Development at the Grand Central Passenger Terminal in New York." *Railway Review*, vol. 68, no. 6, February 5, 1921: 201.

"Clock Man." *New Yorker*, April 27, 1940: 14.

"Commodore Vanderbilt—Erection of a Colossal Bronze Statue, with Allegorical Accessories—A Prodigious Work of Art." *New York Times*, September 2, 1869.

"Commodore Vanderbilt and His Elephant." *Real Estate Record and Builder's Guide*, vol. 9, no. 204, February 10, 1872: 62.

"Connections." *New Yorker*, August 8, 1925: 3.

Consolidated Gas Company of New York and its Affiliated Gas and Electric Companies, Annual Report, 1927: 23.

Coronet, 1946: 17.

Cotter, Holland. "Art in Review." *New York Times*, July 21, 1995: C23.

"Credit Enough for All Concerned." *New York Times*, letter to the editor from Alfred Fellheimer, November 22, 1926.

Croffut, W.A. "William H. Vanderbilt." *American Magazine, Frank Leslie's Popular Monthly*, vol. 21, Jan–June 1886: 135.

"De Luxe." *New Yorker*, July 9, 1932: 10.

Depew, Chauncey Mitchell. *My Memories of Eighty Years*. New York: Charles Scribner's & Sons, 1921.

"Developments at the Grand Central Terminal In New York." *Railway Review*, vol. 57, no. 8, August 21, 1915: 234.

"The Diary of a New Yorker." *Atlanta Constitution*, May 4, 1928: 10.

"Electric Power in Tunnels." *New York Times*, November 7, 1901: 8.

Esterow, Milton. "Terminal to Lose Its 'Mr. Courtesy'; Station Master Who Has Run Grand Central For Eleven Year Retiring at 65." *New York Times*, August 22, 1958.

"Extending the Big Depot: The Grand Central to be Enlarged." *New-York Tribune*, February 19, 1884.

Fabricant, Florence. "Grand Central Palazzo." *New York Times*, November 26, 1997: F9.

"Façade of the Terminal the Keynote to the Structure." *New York Times*, February 2, 1913.

Federal Writers' Publication, Inc. *New York City Guide*. American Guide Series, vol. 1, 1939.

"Fifty Years He Watched the Growth of Grand Central; George Schuman, Now Retiring, Began Work at the Terminal When It Was Called 'the Commodore's Barn' and Had Only 13 Tracks." *New York Times*, June 1, 1924.

"First Electric Train at the Grand Central." *New York Times*, October 1, 1906.

Fischer, Barbara E. Scott. "Cape Cod Fashions Stop Grand Central Train Rush: Hosts at Luncheon Special Edition Delivered Extra Car for Models Style Show Continues." *Christian Science Monitor*, June 11, 1948.

Fiske, Stephen. *Off-Hand Portraits of Prominent New Yorkers*. New York: Geo. R. Lockwood & Son, 1884.

"40-Year Bolshevik Record Shown at Grand Central." *New York Times*, January 21, 1958: 3.

"Frescoes Portray Modern Industry; Artist Paints Vaulted Ceiling Between Graybar Building and Grand Central. Lies On His Back To Work Railroading, Electricity, Radio and Steel Construction Among His Subjects." *New York Times*, March 20, 1927: 7.

"The Gods on the Clock: The Greatest Group of Sculptures in America." *Current Opinion*, August 1914: 133.

"Gone." *New Yorker*, February 26, 1944: 19.

"The Grand Central Art Galleries." *New York Times*, March 21, 1923: 16.

"Grand Central Billboard Going Electric." *New York Times*, January 13, 1967.

"Grand Central Depot Signal System." *Scientific American*, vol. 33, no. 26, December 25, 1875.

"Grand Central Development Seen as Great Civic Center." *Engineering News-Record*, vol. 85, no. 11, September 9, 1920: 501–502.

Grand Central Station Radio Drama (Opening Theme). Radio.

"The Grand Central Station." *New York Times*, August 30, 1897.

"The Grand Central Station Terminal Improvements." *Scientific American,* vol. 93, no. 12, September 16, 1905: 222.

"The Great St. Pancras Railway Station." *Scientific American,* vol. 21, no. 24, December 11, 1869: 376.

"The Grand Central Terminal Building." *Architecture and Building,* vol. 45, no. 4, April 1913: 154.

"Grand Central Terminal." *Freight: The Shippers' Forum,* vol. 11, no. 8, August 1910: 225.

"The Grand Central Terminal—A Great Civic Development." *Engineering News-Record,* vol. 85, no. 11, September 9, 1920: 484.

"Grand Central Terminal—New York City." *Railway and Engineering Review,* vol. 53, no. 4, January 25, 1913: 78.

"Grand Central Terminal Restaurant." *Railroad Reporter and Traveler's News,* vol. 8, no. 2, February 1913: 9.

"The Great Railway Terminal of the Future: 'It Will Be a Way Station,' Says Whitney Warren, Chief Architect of the Grand Central." *New York Times,* February 9, 1913: SM9.

"'Green Caps' to Help Forgetful Travelers." *New York Times,* June 25, 1922.

Grynbaum, Michael. "The Zoo That Is Grand Central, at Full Gallop." *New York Times,* November 26, 2009.

Halloway, Laura Carter. *Famous American Fortunes and the Men Who Have Made Them.* Philadelphia: Bradley & Company, 1884.

Harper's Young People, May 23, 1893.

Hasset, William D. "Off the Record with F.D.R., 1942–1945" (the private diary of Roosevelt's aide William D. Hassett): 281.

"Heine Boiler Tests at Terminal Stations." *Power,* vol. 37, no. 20, May 20, 1913: 702.

"The Helleu Ceiling—More English Portraits—Egypt." *New-York Tribune,* February 16, 1913: A6.

"Herman Offerman has Complete Charge of the 80-Acre Maze of Railroad Track in Grand Central Terminal." *Pittsburgh Press,* March 4, 1938: 23.

"Holds Poor Opinion of American Art: M. Coutan, French Sculptor, has No Desire to Visit This Country." *New York Times,* March 31, 1912: C5.

"Holland Writes of Colossal Railway Projects of New York." *Washington Post,* January 25, 1913: 100.

"Home of Big Auto shows." *The Washington Post,* Feb 12 1911.

"Hotel Commodore, New York. Part I. The General Aspect of the Hotel." *Architecture and Building,* vol. 51, no. 4, April 1919: 1.

Howe, Samuel. "Decoration, Realistic and Impressionistic." *Town and Country,* November 23, 1912.

Hungerford, Edward. "The Greatest Railway Terminal in the World." *Outlook,* December 28, 1912: 905.

"An Innovation." *Morning Herald,* Gloversville and Johnstown, New York, October 5, 1946: 4.

"In the Waiting Room: Red Grooms for Openers." *New York Times,* March 7, 1993: R1.

"An Inspection Party at the New Terminal." *Town and Country,* January 25, 1913: 30.

Kisselgoff, Anna. "Dance: Multimedia and Multilevel Event at Grand Central." *New York Times,* October 11, 1987: 95.

LaFrance, Ernest. "Taming of the Iron Horse." *New York Times,* September 10, 1939.

"Lehman Welcomed to City By Throng." *New York Times,* October 31, 1938: 5.

Letter from engineer Gustav Lindenthal, December 21, 1910.

Letter from "W.J. Wilgus, Fifth Vice President" to "Mr. W.H. Newman, President," March 19, 1903.

Letter to Wilgus on his resignation by New York Central Vice-President Brown, July 5, 1907.

"A Look at the World's Week." *Life,* vol. 43, no. 4, July 22, 1957: 33.

"Lucius Beebe: Twelve Years in New York." *Washington Post,* September 21, 1941: L3.

Markland, John. "Rail Travelers See War Effort." *New York Times,* April 19, 1942: D2

Marshall, David. *Grand Central.* 1946.

"Massive Sculptures if City's Newest Station." *New-York Tribune,* May 31, 1914: D7.

Massock, Richard. "About New York." *Niagara Falls Gazette,* June 27, 1929: 13.

"A Master with Time on His Mind: 41 Years on the Job Tick, Tock, Whir, Hum Checking in the Morning." *New York Times,* April 25, 1980.

McFadden, Robert D. "Fire Wrecks the Oyster Bar, Tiled Oasis at Grand Central." *New York Times,* June 30, 1997: B1.

McFadden, Robert, "Jackie, New Yorker: Friends Recall a Fighter for Her City." *New York Times,* May 22, 1994.

McManus, John T. "Big Doings at the Depot." *New York Times,* May 9, 1937: X3.

"Mecca for Millions." *Popular Mechanics,* vol. 82, no. 5, November 1944: 33–35.

Miller, James. *Miller's New York as It Is, or Stranger's Guide-Book to the Cities of New York, Brooklyn and Adjacent Places.* New York: James Miller, 1880.

Mourey, Gabriel. "Paul Helleu." *Parisian Illustrated Review,* vol. 10, January, 1901.

"Moving a Substation Underground." *Scientific American,* vol. 142, no. 6, June 1930.

"Moving Terminal Power Plant Unique Engineering Feat." *New York Central Lines Magazine,* March 1930.

"Music at Grand Central; Organ Will Be Played Four Hours Daily This Week." *New York Times,* March 24, 1937: 27.

Nanson, Richard W. "By Way of Report." *New York Times,* September 7, 1958: X9.

"The New Grand Central Terminal." *Town and Country,* July 8, 1911: 18.

"The New Grand Central Terminal." *The Independent,* March 14, 1912: 550.

"New York's Grand Central Terminal Gets Decoration." *Christian Science Monitor,* August 8, 1914: 7.

"The New Grand Central Terminal in New York." *Bankers' Magazine,* vol. 86, no. 1, January 1913: 41.

"New Grand Central Opens Its Doors." *New York Times,* February 2, 1913.

"New Grand Central Green Caps Banish All Trouble for a Dime: Placate Wife When Husband Misses Train, Get Theater Tickets, Find Lost Persons and Wake Up Telephone Operators, Some of Their Duties." *New-York Tribune,* July 2, 1922: 4.

"New Highway Runs through a Skyscraper." *Popular Science,* April 1928: 52.

"New Home for Art to Cost $100,000." *New York Times,* March 11, 1923: E7.

"New Item Introduced at Food Conference." *Long Island Star-Journal,* October 7, 1954.

"News of General Interest in the Secular World." *Herald of Gospel Liberty,* September 16, 1915: 1170.

"The New Railroad Depot at Forty-Second Street and Fourth Avenue." *Scientific American,* vol. 25, no. 3, July 15, 1871: 40.

"The New Union Depot." *Real Estate Record and Builder's Guide,* vol. 6, no.138, November 5, 1870: 3.

New York Tribune, October 3, 1897.

"News of the Railroads: New Waiting Room at the Grand Central Station Opens To-day. Appointments Are Up to Date and Improvements of a Modern Type—Some Novel Ideas." *New York Times,* October 18, 1900.

New York Evening Telegram, March 14, 1872.

Newsday, January 20, 1987: 3.

"The New Vanderbilt Depot-Progress of the Work." *New York Times,* December 8, 1870: 6.

"New Waldorf Gets Own Rail Siding." *New York Times,* September 8, 1929.

New Yorker, August 1, 1925: 10.

New Yorker, January 21, 1928: 28.

New York Times, December 3, 1989: 94.

"Of Local Origin." *New York Times,* August 22, 1958: 14.

"Old Grand Central to Disappear Soon." *New York Times,* March 15, 1910: 11.

"One Signal Tower Controls Seventy-Nine Acres of Track." *New York Times,* February 2, 1913.

On Track: The Monthly News Publication for Metro-North Employees, November 1986.

On Track: The Monthly News Publication for Metro-North Employees, February 1992.

"On Videotape... From New York... The Underground Party That Was." *Herald Tribune,* 1965.

"Open Big Biltmore on New Year's Eve; Newest of the City's Great Hotels Has Novel Features. It Has Cost $10,000,000 Has Direct Connection with the Grand Central Terminal: 1,000 Rooms for Guests." *New York Times,* December 26, 1913.

"Optimism is Urged by Mrs. Roosevelt." *New York Times,* December 2, 1932: 23.

"The Oyster Season Begins Tomorrow." New York Times, August 31, 1950: 20.

Paddleford, Clementine. "Oyster Season." *Atlanta Constitution*, September 3, 1944: 16.

Paddleford, Clementine. "New York, N.Y.: His Majesty, The Oyster." *Los Angeles Times*, December 18, 1949: H21.

"Parade will Mark Park Av. Opening: Property Owners to Celebrate Completed Thoroughfare Next Wednesday. Less Traffic Strain On 5th Borough President Dowling Tells What This Street Means to City Traffic. Vehicular Roadway Built." *New York Times*, April 13, 1919.

"Park Av. Tunnel Enters New Era; As Automobile Highway It Will Perform Service for Still Another Kind of Travel." *New York Times*, September 15, 1935.

"Pershing Arrives for Sons Wedding." *New York Times*, April 21, 1938.

"Plans Finest Home For Californian: French Architect Returning After a Study of Mrs. Carolan's 1,000-Acre Estate." *New York Times*, December 26, 1912: 6.

"Playground Virtuosos in Concert." *New York Times*, August 23, 1988: B1.

"Proceedings of the Tenth Annual Convention of the American Institute of Architects." Boston, Franklin Press: 1876.

"Progress of Rapid Transit in New York City." *Scientific American*, vol. 32, no. 23, June 5, 1875: 352.

"Preparing Block for New Waldorf." *New York Times*, March 31, 1929.

"Progress on the Grand Central Terminal." *Railway Age Gazette*, vol. 53, no. 21, November 22, 1912: 983.

"President Has No Comment; Returns on Special Train." *New York Times*, July 27, 1951.

"Pullman Reservation Bureau, G.C.T., Is Sound Proofed and Air Conditioned." *New York Central Headlight*, vol. 6, no. 6, June 1945: 12.

"Questions of the Traveler." *New York Times*, June 11, 1916.

"Rats." *The New Yorker*, September 9, 1933.

"Railroad Offers New Exhibit Here." *New York Times*, February 18, 1948: 3.

Railway Age Gazette, October 7, 1910.

Railway Gazette, December 1889.

"Railway Industries." *Railway World*, vol. 24, Quarto vol. 6, no. 32, August 7, 1880: 749.

Railway Review, February 5, 1921: 201.

"Rainbow Division Off: National Guardsman to Leave for Two Weeks in Field." *New York Times*, July 8, 1955: 26.

Real Estate Record and Builder's Guide, vol. 3, no. 64, June 5, 1869: 4.

"Reconstruction of the Grand Central Station in New York City." *American Engineer Car Builder and Railroad Journal*, vol. 71, 1897: 104.

"Relief Needed in Park-Ave." *New York Tribune*, July 2, 1901.

"Remarkable Development Of Park Avenue South Of Fifty-Second Street In Last Six Years Graphically Illustrated By Pictorial Contrast." *New York Times*, June 26, 1921: 94.

"Run, Dance, and Be Noisy." *New York Times*, January 5, 1992: 33.

"Safer New Year's Pressed in Nation." *New York Times*, December 31, 1955.

"Sales of Bonds Advocated: Huge Photo-Mural in Grand Central Terminal Dedicated." *New York Times*, December 15, 1941: 33.

Santora, Marc. "Teeth Missing? Try Lost and Found: At Grand Central, Even Dentures Have Been Reclaimed." *New York Times*, August 20, 2002.

"Sargent as a Modern Master in His Retrospective Show: Stirring From the First The Higginson Portrait Some Old Bogies A Who's Who Roster." *Christian Science Monitor*, March 3, 1924: 11.

Shepard, Richard. "Actor to Portray Eishenhower on TV." *New York Times*, November 19, 1955: 39.

"The Sky Line." *New Yorker*, December 15, 1928: 119.

"Some Aspects of Training and Design." *British Architect*, March 8, 1907: 165.

Souvenir and Official Programme of the Press Club Fair: Grand Central Palace, New York, May 1893: 9.

"Strange Finds on Trains." *New York Times*, September 19, 1920.

Stein, Sonia. "CBS to Build Huge Television Plant in N.Y." *Washington Post*, February 22, 1948: L3.

Stern, Michael. "Political Activism New Hippie 'Thing'." *New York Times*, March 24, 1968: 1.

"Terminal to Mark 25th Anniversary." *New York Times*, January 30, 1938.

Thompson, Hugh. "The Greatest Railroad Terminal in the World." *Munsey's Magazine*, vol. 45, no. 1, April 1911: 27.

"Time Out for Clock; Grand Central Timepiece takes First 'Break' for Repairs." *New York Times*, January 17, 1954.

"Truman Arrives; Continues Attacks on General Here." *New York Times*, October 11, 1952.

"The Tunnel Slaughter." *New York Times*, January 9, 1902.

"Underground Power House." *New York Times*, December 1, 1929.

"Under the Biltmore Clock: It Is Favorite Place for College Dating." *Life*, April 21, 1952: 158.

"The Vanderbilt Railroad Depot in New York." *The Railroad Gazette*, July 15, 1871: 176.

"Vanderbilt's As Home Builders." *New York Times*, October 12, 1902.

Van Gelder, Lawrence. "Going Out Guide." *New York Times*, August 29, 1972: 22.

"Vast Transit Links Will Be Beneath Commodore Hotel: Guests Will Experience No Difficulty in Travelling to Places in Greater City." *New-York Tribune*, May 20, 1917.

Wald, Matthew. "Parcel Room Lost & Found; Grand Central Finds Treasure and Trash Left by Commuters." *New York Times*, April 4, 1978.

"The Waldorf Again." *The Architect*, vol. 13, 1929: 103.

"What's Lost is Found in New York Exhibit." *Christian Science Monitor*, May 19, 1995: 15.

Whitney Warren, quoted in *The Sun*, February 2, 1913.

"And Who Wants Job Answering All of These?" *The Atlanta Constitution*, December 22, 1930.

William Wilgus, Record of the Inception and Creation of the Grand Central Terminal Improvement, 1902–1913.

Winchester, James H. "Grand Central's no. 17 World's Busiest Phone Booth: Did You Know U.S. Collects $325 Million Yearly From Its Telephones?" *Christian Science Monitor*, October 30, 1964: 13.

"With the Surrounding Buildings It Covers an Area of Thirty City Blocks—Can Accommodate 100,000,000 People A Year." *New York Times*, February 2, 1913.

Wolters, Larry. "News Radio." *Chicago Daily Tribune*, August 24, 1937: 18.

"Woman Organist Reaches Throng Of Travelers With Her Music: Many Boys Grateful Seemed Like Home." *Christian Science Monitor*, December 24, 1943: 14.

"Wonders Grow Near New Grand Central: Work Will Cost $180,000,000 and a New Park Avenue Will Rise to the North." *New York Times*, June 26, 1910: C5.

Writers Guide to New York City, 1939.

"Xmas Mail Moves Fast, Morgan Says." *New York Times*, December 21, 1913: 8.

Yarrow, Andrew L. "Adventurous Performers in Unexpected Places." *New York Times*, October 9, 1987: H18.

Yarrow, Andrew L. "Even Offstage, These Performers Are Onstage." *New York Times*, October 4, 1987.

"Yuletide Caroling Arrives on Schedule at Two Big Railroad Terminals Here." *New York Times*, December 11, 1956: 42.

INDEX

ACKNOWLEDGMENTS

The Transit Museum's research team, led by archivist Carey Stumm and associate archivist Brett Dion, were relentless in their determination, enthusiastic in their resourcefulness, and immediate in their responsiveness. Their ability to find anything and everything formed the foundation of this book. The exquisite and prolific photography of Frank English, Metro North's photographer for twenty-six years, inspired us to believe we could create a book on Grand Central different from those that preceded ours. Frank took a long-term government job and made it art. Patrick Cashin's equally beautiful photos were created in his role as Metropolitan Transportation Authority's current photographer. We are grateful to Tony Robins for his role in structuring the book, for bringing it to life with voices from the past, and for his clarity of thought and prose. And Tony Hiss set the gold standard for both vision and turn of phrase.

Railroad careers seem to engender longevity. Consequently, we were lucky to have the collective years of expertise of the following Metro North employees and retirees: Margie Anders, Dan Brucker, Peter Crawford, Randy Fleischer, Janek Kozlowski, George Monasterio, Sal Oliva, Bob Saraceni, R. L. Smith, Michael Stetson, Mike Vitiello, Bob Walker, and George Walker.

We are grateful to the many institutions and repositories that loaned us materials from their collections and shared their knowledge with us. They are noted in credits throughout the book, though we would like to specially mention Erik Huber, Linda Briscoe Myers, Tal Nadan, Mark Renovitch, and our own Desiree Alden. We note with gratitude the generosity of the following sister institutions: the FDR Library, Harry Ransom Center, Museum of the City of New York, New-York Historical Society, New York Public Library, New York State Archives, New York Yacht Club, the New Yorker, and the New York Times.

Private collectors and historians, also generous in sharing their passion, include Jim Greller, Herbert Harwood, Roderick Kennedy, Frederique de Watrigant, Cathy Horn, photographer Gerald Weinstein, and writer Christopher Gray.

It is amazing how much nonprofit work gets done by interns. Ours were Zack Chauvin, Peri Pignetti, Mariko Saito, and Jaime Sheehan. We know they all have brilliant futures ahead of them.

Special thanks to our agent, Noah Lukeman of Lukeman Literary Management, for believing in us and coaching us through our third book. We thank the team at Stewart, Tabori & Chang, especially our editor Jennifer Levesque. And Roy Rub and Seth Labenz of Topos Graphics made this book the stunner we knew it could be, and patiently walked us through each phase of design. A grant toward the production of this book was generously provided by Furthermore, a program of the J.M. Kaplan Fund.

Finally, we are grateful to the Metropolitan Transportation Authority, Joseph Lhota, chairman, and Metro-North Railroad, Howard Permut, president, for their support of the Transit Museum and the Grand Central Terminal Centennial celebration. We appreciate their giving us the freedom to develop and prioritize content on the agencies' vast and significant history.